UNHOLY TRINITY

UNHOLY TRINITY

The hunt for the paedophile priest
Monsignor John Day

DENIS RYAN and **PETER HOYSTED**

ALLEN&UNWIN
SYDNEY・MELBOURNE・AUCKLAND・LONDON

First published in 2013

Copyright © Denis Ryan and Peter Hoysted 2013

All rights reserved. No part of this book may be reproduced or transmitted in any form or by any means, electronic or mechanical, including photocopying, recording or by any information storage and retrieval system, without prior permission in writing from the publisher. The Australian *Copyright Act 1968* (the Act) allows a maximum of one chapter or 10 per cent of this book, whichever is the greater, to be photocopied by any educational institution for its educational purposes provided that the educational institution (or body that administers it) has given a remuneration notice to Copyright Agency Limited (CAL) under the Act.

Allen & Unwin

83 Alexander Street
Crows Nest NSW 2065
Australia

Phone: (61 2) 8425 0100
Email: info@allenandunwin.com
Web: www.allenandunwin.com

Cataloguing-in-Publication details are available
from the National Library of Australia
www.trove.nla.gov.au

ISBN 978 1 74331 402 9

Set in 12.5/17 pt Bembo by Post Pre-press Group, Australia
Printed and bound in Australia by Griffin Press

10 9 8 7 6 5 4 3 2 1

MIX
Paper from responsible sources
FSC® C009448

The paper in this book is FSC® certified. FSC® promotes environmentally responsible, socially beneficial and economically viable management of the world's forests.

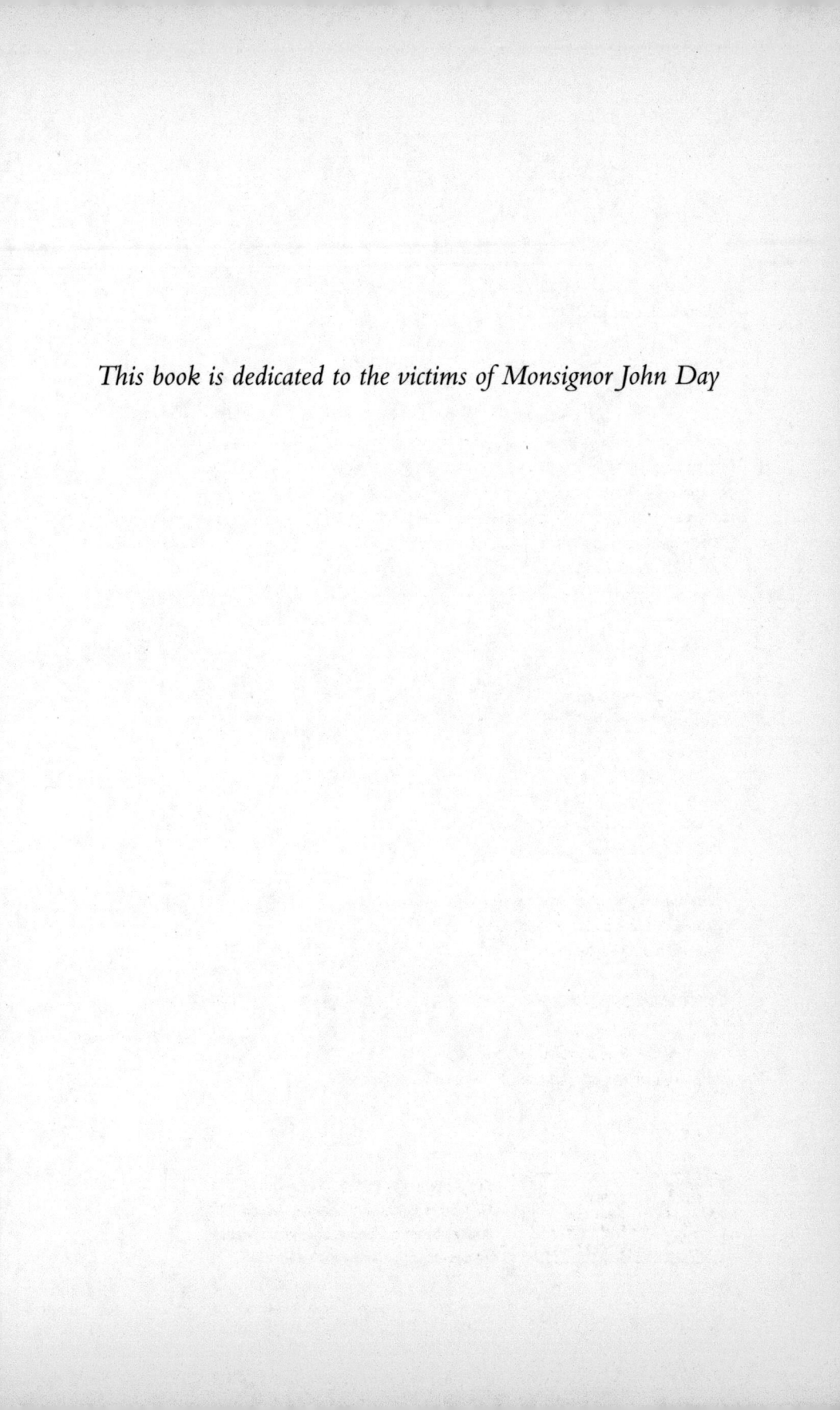

This book is dedicated to the victims of Monsignor John Day

AUTHORS' NOTE

No doubt some will say that this book reveals a streak of anti-Catholicism—a pernicious attack on the faith and a certain sign of the deeply embedded prejudices of its authors. However, it is the authors' belief that the Roman Catholic Church is fundamentally a force for good in this world.

Yet in this story lies a tale of almost unimaginable depravity committed by one of the Church's foot soldiers. That Monsignor John Day, the priest discussed in this book, was a prolific criminal and Australia's worst sex offender is indisputable. What is not known and must be understood is that Day could only have plumbed these sordid depths with the active collusion of members of the Roman Catholic Church and elements of the Victoria Police force. The default setting for both institutions was to protect the image and reputation of the Roman Catholic Church, and to be dismissive of Day's sins, without regard for his victims. By their collusion, these institutions unleashed a psychopath on unsuspecting communities—a psychopath who could offend at will and without fear of the consequences. Even when his behaviour became widely known, Day was merely placed into temporary exile, and his crimes hushed up before he could return to prey yet again on children.

This book is called *Unholy Trinity* because, while Day raped and assaulted children alone, his evil could only have continued with the support of an active conspiracy involving police and the legal system. In Mildura in the 1950s, '60s and '70s, the other members of the triumvirate were a senior detective, James Barritt, and a clerk of the courts, Joseph Kearney. These three men rode roughshod over Mildura for thirteen years. Any attempt to bring a member of the triumvirate to justice was met with fearful retribution from the other two. They created an almost unshakeable structure that allowed the three men to pervert the course of justice and intimidate the community with impunity.

More widely, elements of the Victoria Police force would be called on to do their duty—not to the citizenry they served but, in the words of a police detective who tried to recruit Denis Ryan into this shadowy group, 'to defend the Cathedral'. In the force's black humour, it became known as 'the Catholic Mafia'. It is hard to understand why these policemen took the directions they did and perverted the course of justice for the sake of themselves and their religion. What these police officers did was, in itself, criminal. The fact is that there were no consequences for the perpetrators of these crimes within the force because the perpetrators were also the investigators.

AUTHORS' NOTE

The evidence of complicity at senior levels of the Church hierarchy is overpowering. It has broken not only the criminal law codes but also its own canon law. The crimes committed by Monsignor John Day were not only a state felony but also a mortal sin, according to the Church's own teachings. It is hoped that this book will make people question why the Church sanctioned sexual crimes against its children by some of its priests. These crimes involve the most disgusting and sickening acts against children.

Finally, we would like to point out that we have protected the identity of many of Day's victims by not giving their real names, and also by changing some of their personal details.

DENIS RYAN AND PETER HOYSTED

FOREWORD

This is a saga of intrigue, stupidity, incomprehensible behaviour and heroism.

More particularly it is the story of the stoical bravery of Denis Ryan in the face of a trinity of resistance from his own department, the Catholic Church and his own generally apathetic community.

It raises the moral issue of a church that demands unquestioning obedience from its clergy and adherents; the status and validity of canon law over the civil code; and the preservation of the reputation, and moral authority, of the Church against the interest, and welfare, of the victims of a paedophile priest.

It questions the logic, morality and judgment of transferring an offending priest into a similar professional environment with his sexual proclivities unsupervised, thereby providing a further occasion to offend. This in the pious expectation that

FOREWORD

the reformative would run some natural course and God's servant would be restored to virtue.

Denis Ryan is a very courageous and determined man. In his career as a police officer he never wavered from the strongly held belief that no person is above, or beyond, the law. His veneration of this maxim cost Denis his career, his marriage and his faith.

An exemplary and practising Catholic, he first encountered his nemesis John Day in disgraceful circumstances in the streets of St Kilda in 1956. This first meeting was a test of his belief in the universal goodness of all clergy and all things Catholic, and in the above stated maxim. It was a rude awakening for the young, conflicted constable.

How the paths of the two men collided in spectacular fashion many years after the St Kilda meeting, and how others became enmeshed in this complex and squalid story, is the stuff of fiction.

Yet it is no fiction. This story is the true and honest account of one man's frustration and eventual despair as he tried to bring a cruel and malicious man to appropriate justice.

It is a story that examines the culpability of high-ranking police officers, who should have known better; people of God who acted covertly, reprehensibly and unlawfully, to protect one priest and the status of the Church and in doing so wreaked untold damage to its cause.

And it is a story of the specific damage and distress that these so-called men of the law and of God caused their respective institutions in their attempts to cover up the rot at their core.

More importantly, perhaps, it is a story that, while specifically dealing with this one incident, gives rise to all sorts of questions about the extent of the rot and the damage caused throughout the wider community.

Denis Ryan was also damaged as a result of this harrowing and brutal saga. In his eighty-second year now, he is a man around which the demons of stress and panic hover closely. He has suffered immensely over the decades because he knows that in the thwarting of his investigation, greater suffering was caused to those much more vulnerable and defenceless than he.

Denis Ryan emerges untarnished from this harrowing saga. We should all be grateful to this brave and persistent man, who by his revelations has contributed to making us better people and the world a better place. In the words of Robert F. Kennedy in his eulogy to Martin Luther King Jr: 'To tame the savageness of man and make gentle the life of this world.'

BRYAN HARDING
Chief Superintendent Victoria Police (Ret.)
Secretary Victoria Police Association (former)
February 2013

CONTENTS

Authors' note	vii
Foreword	x
Prologue: An extraordinary coincidence	1
1 On the beat	11
2 Ditching the uniform	25
3 The deep north	48
4 Confessions	81
5 Power without glory	118
6 The Catholic Mafia	133
7 The smother	150
8 A brush with scandal	181
9 Bloodied but unbowed	210
Afterword	222
Day and the darkness: three victims speak	225
Acknowledgments	254
Index	257

PROLOGUE:
AN EXTRAORDINARY COINCIDENCE

*They have learned nothing
and forgotten nothing.*
TALLEYRAND, 1754–1838

I'm Dinny Ryan and I have just turned 81 years of age.

God only knows how the events described in this book happened. Were they preordained? I am a man of unwavering faith in my God, so I have to believe that I was destined to clash with the paedophile priest, Monsignor John Day.

Others will call it a matter of coincidence. If that's the case, it was an extraordinary one.

I collided with Monsignor John Day twice. The first time was on the streets of St Kilda in inner city Melbourne when I was in the company of two fellow uniform police officers. Day—drunk to the eyeballs, his cock out—was with a couple of well known prostitutes from the area. That was in 1956. I was barely out of the academy. The second time was in 1971, when I was a detective stationed in Mildura, in north-west Victoria on the Murray River. I'd conducted an investigation into Day's paedophilia. I found witnesses and obtained statements from his victims. I had him banged to rights. But on both occasions Day walked away.

John Michael Joseph Day was already a priest when I was born in 1931. He had made his way through the Corpus Christi College in Werribee, a shining edifice for the future priesthood established by that great defender of the Catholic faith, Archbishop Daniel Mannix. At the Victorian parliamentary inquiry into child sex abuse, Professor Des Cahill from RMIT prepared a submission that revealed that, of the 378 priests who graduated from Corpus Christi between 1940 and 1966, 14 have been convicted of child sexual abuse and 4 more, who have since gone to meet their God, were also abusers. By my rough arithmetic that's 1 in 20—about forty times the number of sex offenders in the general community.

Day isn't included in these statistics, because he graduated from Corpus Christi in 1927. He was assigned to his first parish, Colac, near Geelong, in 1936, having spent the preceding years as a young priest at Ballarat East. Day rarely moved out of the Ballarat diocese from that time on. The diocese stretches from Portland in the south-west through to Bacchus Marsh and north through Ballarat and Bendigo all the way up to Mildura, excepting Geelong and Melbourne.

After Colac, Day was sent to Ararat, then Horsham, Beech Forest and Apollo Bay before being dispatched to Mildura. There he spent fifteen years, standing over the community, helping himself to parishioners' money, committing complex fraud and wantonly raping children. While I wouldn't learn of his crimes until 1971, I have since discovered that Day was an active paedophile throughout most, if not all, of his

PROLOGUE: AN EXTRAORDINARY COINCIDENCE

priestly existence. He preyed on hundreds of victims and committed thousands of offences.

Day and I grew up worlds apart. He was born in Warrnambool twenty-seven years before me. I was born in Sydney and raised in a household that took an even view of religion. My mother, Emily, was a Seventh Day Adventist. My father, Francis, had endured the worst humanity had to offer on the fields of Flanders. He was on the front lines in the Somme for a year and a half before a bomb exploded in his trench, the shrapnel tearing his knee apart. He didn't have much truck with religion after that.

Life was hard for the family in Depression-era Australia and my mother turned to the nuns at St Finbar's in Sans Souci for support. The nuns were kind to her and as a result I was raised a Catholic. Even though I would learn that some priests behaved disgracefully and some criminally, I have remained a Roman Catholic and I will die a Roman Catholic.

I served as a detective in the Victoria Police force for sixteen years. By the time I transferred to Mildura, I'd investigated and charged murderers, rapists, vicious gunmen. I'd been shot at, stabbed and on one occasion even kidnapped by the Melbourne hoodlum, Harry 'The Horse' Gribbin. But I'd never come across anything like the situation I found in Mildura—Monsignor John Day, the parish priest, was at the centre of an evil that defied human understanding.

That a man, let alone a priest and, in Day's case, a monsignor (a colonel in the Catholic army) could commit crimes of such violence against children challenged my faith and cost me the job I loved. This man used his office as a means of enforcing his sexual perversity on young children.

He raped, sodomised and committed acts of gross indecency on children as young as eight.

For the victims, it was not just the pain of rape and sexual assault. These children were deeply traumatised, their lives set on a road to oblivion. There were suicides and lives lost in reckless abandon; other children were dispatched to a living hell of trauma and sorrow.

As a spiritual adviser to his flock, Day was able to wield his perverse influence. He imposed himself upon parents who believed him to be a man beyond mortal sin. The children he raped kept their silence. He threatened and bullied them into submission. They understood the power he held over them, knowing they would not be believed.

It did not occur to the vast majority of people, be they parishioners or those out of the spiritual reach of the Church, that a Catholic priest would behave in this way. I suppose it was just too difficult to contemplate. At first, I did not believe it either and, when I did, I found it almost impossible to comprehend.

Day's victims were easy to find, though they were often reluctant to speak, at least at first. They felt a victim's shame of the crimes perpetrated upon them, and dreaded someone uncovering Day's dark secrets. They understood the power of the Catholic Church and that they were powerless to challenge it. They felt alone.

The allegations of sexual assaults and rape against Day became known to me by increment. First one victim, then another and then more came forward until I had the evidence to charge him. These people had courage—that rarest of commodities in today's world. Sometimes their parents had

PROLOGUE: AN EXTRAORDINARY COINCIDENCE

rejected their accusations, adding to their injuries with their own beatings. Other victims who had told their parents were not believed. Most had remained silent.

When I explained to them the magnitude of Day's depravity and how his crimes threatened to turn more lives on end, the victims understood that this creature's crimes must come to an end and that he must be brought to justice. Ultimately, twelve people provided signed statements detailing rape and abuse at the hands of Day.

As a police officer, I had been given a bird's eye view of the dark side of the human spirit. I had investigated child sex offenders previously and put them away. But the detail provided in the statements gave me an ugly view of these offences. I could see Day preying on these children. I could envisage him touching, fondling and raping these kids. I felt their terror at the realisation of what was happening to them. My blood boiled.

I flirted with the thought of fronting Day on the steps of the presbytery and belting him around the head with a lump of four by two. I was capable of it—I had belted plenty of crooks. And he was a crook, but much worse than the standover men and violent bastards I had encountered in Melbourne.

My real interest—and some have described it as an obsession—was to bring Day to account for his manifest cruelties and the lives that he had effectively destroyed.

The Catholic Church weighed heavily over many of our lives and it brooked no argument. The Church is two thousand years old and the oldest manifestation of Christianity, but in many ways it behaves like a cult, with its charismatic leadership and forced disconnection for followers who have been judged to have strayed from the path. Its authority pervades from cradle to grave.

The Catholic education system in Australia has made a unique contribution to the intellectual and academic life of the nation. Yet at a spiritual level it has churned out proselytes—many with a zealot's gleam in their eyes. These people have emerged in positions of authority—in government, in the judicial system, in all levels of bureaucracy and in the police. These people—some of them great, most of them good—preferred not to contemplate that the Church's gatekeepers—its parish priests—could commit these crimes against children. Whether it was through fear or other forms of control, Catholics could not see the wood for the trees.

In some cases, they did know and chose to do nothing or, in the most egregious cases, they acted as the Church's foot soldiers, protecting priests like Day from examination.

Day believed that he had been ordained by a superior power to be the supervisor of our morals, but he was a man without the first semblance of morality. He may have joined the Church despite his unconstrained sexual perversions, or perhaps because of them. What he knew implicitly was that the authority that came with being a priest verged on the absolute; his crimes against children were unlikely to be exposed.

While Day acted out his depravities on his own, he did so under the protection of the Catholic Church. Bishop James Patrick O'Collins had been Day's mentor within the Ballarat diocese, one that unleashed an epidemic of paedophilia—more often than not from Day and Gerald Ridsdale, a self-confessed child rapist and paedophile priest.

PROLOGUE: AN EXTRAORDINARY COINCIDENCE

Ridsdale raped and assaulted hundreds of victims in western Victoria. Whenever the allegations started heaping up against him, the Church simply transferred him. In the 1970s and 1980s he committed thousands of crimes against children across Australia and around the world. In 1994 he was convicted of numerous counts of buggery, indecent assault and gross indecency, and sentenced to eighteen years in prison. As more victims came forward, he faced additional charges, and in 2006 he pleaded guilty to further counts of buggery and sexual assault. His non-parole sentence was extended by four years in 2006.

Day and Ridsdale were the worst sex criminals this nation has seen. They were able to commit their crimes because the diocese chose to obfuscate, frustrate and obstruct any attempt to have them brought to justice. They were free to commit their abominations because they had the active protection of their bishop.

When complaints against paedophile priests became too loud, Bishop O'Collins moved them on to new districts and new parishes, where Day and Ridsdale, in particular, were able to commit their crimes again. And even though O'Collins knew that Day had raped children in Apollo Bay in the 1950s, he didn't move Day away from angry and disillusioned parishioners and into anonymity. He nurtured and sponsored him, transferred and promoted him, sending him to Mildura, where he was promoted to dean then finally monsignor. When O'Collins retired in 1971, Bishop Ronald Mulkearns replaced him as bishop for the Ballarat diocese.

I admit to many failings in my life. As a detective investigating Day, naivety was one of them, at least at first. I did not anticipate the lengths to which the Catholic Church would go to cover up for one of its own. But as the evidence against Day mounted, I informed Mulkearns. He knew that I had victims' statements. He knew that I had a case against his paedophile priest. But the bishop dismissed the allegations with a haughty wave of his hand. Mulkearns advised that Day had been interviewed by the police and Day's denials were considered enough. The victims were ignored, their pain dismissed as the slander of mischief-makers. And Day was free to continue raping children in Mildura.

But it wasn't just the Church that allowed paedophile priests like Day to continue their sordid conduct unchecked. I later found that a group of police officers, known as the Catholic Mafia, actively suppressed investigations into paedophile priests. Although these officers nominally reported to the chief commissioner, they really owed their allegiance to St Patrick's Cathedral.

Back in the 1960s, two detectives in Brunswick had investigated a priest from the Don Bosco Youth Centre in Sydney Road for child sex offences. I knew one of the detectives well. He told me many years later that he had arrested the priest, and was in the process of placing him in the watch house, when along came Detective Chief Inspector Jim Rosengren, a senior CIB detective based at Russell Street in Melbourne. Rosengren asked one of the detectives what was going on. The detective explained that they were in the process of charging the priest with a string of child sex offences, including buggery. Rosengren, a strident Catholic, told the two detectives that he would take over the investigation. The two detectives were shocked and not a little annoyed by

PROLOGUE: AN EXTRAORDINARY COINCIDENCE

the intrusion. When they queried Rosengren, he said: 'I'm taking over and that's a fucking order.'

And that was that. Nothing ever came of it. The priest was not charged, and was free to go on and commit further crimes against children.

I wondered how it was that Rosengren found himself in that place and at that time. I can only guess that he had been tipped off, either by the Church or by other police at the Brunswick station.

There are many other examples—some not of collusion but of a reluctance to pursue charges against priests. Many senior coppers knew they would be hard against it trying to get a priest to court.

There was Bill Hower, a detective senior constable, who had spent twenty years in the Homicide Squad. He was a decent bloke. In the 1960s, after his tenure in Homicide, he ended up in Horsham, where Day had once been the parish priest. Many years after my battle against Day, the Catholic Church and the coppers who protected him reached a climax, Bill rang me. 'You've got more guts than me, Dinny,' he told me. 'I copped some of this when I got to Horsham but I didn't follow it up.'

Hower was referring to a number of complaints he had received of child sexual abuse perpetrated by Day. Bill had arrived at Horsham after Day had been moved on. He regretted not pursuing Day, but believed that somewhere along the line the Catholic Mafia would intervene and make Bill an offer he could not refuse.

Another case involved Col Mooney, a detective sergeant at Bendigo in 1975. Col had received information that Gerald

Ridsdale had sexually abused a young boy living in the area. Mooney's investigations were stymied when the parents of the boy refused to allow him to be interviewed by police. Col took his concerns to the Catholic hierarchy. The result was that Ridsdale was simply moved along to another parish, where he would prey upon a new group of unsuspecting children.

❖

I always thought I was a city copper. I enjoyed investigating serious crime. I relished the thrill of the hunt. If I'd had a choice I wouldn't have sought a transfer to Mildura to become a country copper. But that decision was more or less made for me.

When I got to Mildura in 1962, I had to make a go of it, because I knew I'd be there for a long time. On my first day on duty in the town, I was shown around by the senior detective in Mildura, an especially bullish sergeant and devout Roman Catholic called Jim Barritt.

Barritt was a hulking man. No amount of warning could have prepared me for meeting him in person. He was 185 centimetres tall and 140 kilograms. His head was huge. A shearer's cook could have squeezed Barritt's head into the pot and made enough soup for the entire shearing season, and still have had plenty left for the dogs afterwards. Standing alongside him, I felt like David to his Goliath. The only problem was I didn't have a slingshot.

Just one day into the job at Mildura, I had Barritt yelling and ranting in my ears, defending Day and belittling me.

Welcome to Mildura, I thought. This is going to be fun.

It wasn't, but at least I'm still alive to tell the tale.

1
ON THE BEAT

Oh! What a tangled web we weave,
When first we practise to deceive.
SIR WALTER SCOTT, 1771–1832

By 1956 I had been a copper for four years, having come to the job through a circuitous path. I'd always wanted to be a police officer but my parents wouldn't let me join up in New South Wales, so I travelled around Australia, finding work where I could before I settled in Melbourne. My grandfather, Thomas, had served in the New South Wales police force and my great uncle, Tighe, had worked his way up the ladder in New South Wales to become a superintendent in the CIB.

At 175 centimetres, I was tall enough to join any force across the country, but my light, 68-kilogram frame was a problem. On the day I applied to join the Victoria Police force, I sat outside the depot and devoured two pounds of bananas in an effort to get my weight up to pass muster. I don't know if the bananas helped, but the scales tipped in my favour and I was in.

Some shifts I found myself stuck at the station, helping out in the watch house, doing paperwork and being the face of the force as people came into the station with complaints. Sometimes I was on watch-house duties, processing the residents of the cells for the night.

The worst shifts had me stuck in what was called files and inquiries—following up motor licences and making inquiries with motor registration and other government departments. The hands on the clock would crawl. Often I looked up at the clock in the station and it seemed like the hands had gone backwards.

Files and inquiries also meant I had to get out on an old police bike to deliver summonses. The police bikes were as heavy as Sherman tanks, with a turning circle to match. As you might expect, I was rarely made welcome. A lot of doors were slammed in my face. It wasn't what I had joined the police force for, but it was all part of being a uniformed police officer learning the ropes.

Each week I checked the noticeboard to see what shifts I'd been given. I preferred to work nights because, more often than not, that would have me out on the divisional van patrols. The divisional vans had radios and we were called in to attend crime scenes by D-24, the radio headquarters based at Russell Street. The divvy patrols could be exhilarating. We were called into anything and everything. Murders, burglaries, punch-ups—any sort of misbehaviour you could imagine.

The old blue Dodge divisional vans didn't have heaters. The powers-that-be thought it might be too dangerous to have us in a van with the heater on. I guess they thought it would put us to sleep, and we might nod off while in pursuit of a speeding vehicle. I learnt pretty quickly to dress in layers when I was due to go out on divvy van patrol—two pairs of socks, two singlets and two vests underneath my police jumper and tunic to ward off the cold.

I had no such worries one balmy Melbourne night in March 1956. I had just my shirt and tunic on, and was out in Divisional Van 10 as it rolled down Wellington Street towards St Kilda Junction. I glanced at my watch. It was just past one. Only one more hour to go and I'd be back at the station, putting my feet up with a cuppa and a sandwich.

I looked across at Senior Constable Tom Jenkins. Tom's face had aged more than its forty-two years. Three years in Changi prisoner-of-war camp will do that. While his face revealed the hardships he'd endured at the hands of Imperial Japan, his body had recovered its strength and power.

Tom's eyes shifted along the road and into the distance, his left elbow dangling casually on the passenger door. He was an experienced copper and his eyes scanned the area looking for anything out of the ordinary. Tom had been working the St Kilda beat for years. He'd seen them come and go—the 'gunnies' and bludgers who ruled the working girls with violence and intimidation, the SPs and sly groggers, the rubber-neckers, the hoons and the hooligans, the desperate and the dangerous.

On my right sat the driver, Constable Clarrie Bell, aged 25, dark hair, well built, clean cut. He was only a year older than me. He'd been through the academy a year earlier and had six months' service ahead of me.

Even in the dark, St Kilda looked like it could do with a lick of paint. The grand Edwardian houses paid for by a long gone gold rush now stood dilapidated. Many had been transformed into boarding houses offering cheap accommodation and anonymity for the itinerants who were drawn to St Kilda like moths to the flame.

The bay-side suburb is eight kilometres from Melbourne's central business district, a twenty-minute trip by tram down St Kilda Road. It had once been a playground for the wealthy. There was the beach, the restaurants and clubs, and Luna Park on the Lower Esplanade, with its giant laughing face facade an open invitation to lovers and giggling children.

A depression and two world wars later and St Kilda had become a playground of a different type—Melbourne's dedicated red light district and a magnet for night crawlers.

Wedged between my two colleagues, my job was lookout. The streets were quiet but I knew the reverie could be shattered in a heartbeat.

As a young uniformed officer at St Kilda, I was doing the hard yards in a tough school, but I was fortunate to be in such good company. My two colleagues were men to watch, admire and emulate. Tom Jenkins, in particular.

The van shuddered and jolted along towards the junction, a spaghetti bowl of roads that converged in St Kilda's heart. In the headlights, I spotted the Ford Crestline crawling along the gutter, the gigantic frame weaving ever closer to the curb. Tom had spotted the car a second or two ahead of me, as usual.

'What's that crazy bastard doing?' he said. On cue, Clarrie accelerated, pulling the divvy van alongside the metal monster.

Tom wound down his window and pointed at the driver. 'Pull over.'

The driver was Hazel Hanrahan, a prostitute known to us all. She had a long criminal record, with a string of convictions for street offences. Her partner and pimp was Bobby Bull, the notorious gunman, painter and docker. The thought of Hazel Hanrahan lurching down the road in a big expensive American car set off the alarm bells for me. It was obvious the car wasn't hers and she had some explaining to do. Hazel rolled the Ford along the curb before it finally came to rest. She waited in the car.

I clambered out of the car with Tom and Clarrie. I knew Hazel wasn't violent but my heart was still pounding. This was what I had joined the force for—the adrenaline rush, the uncertainty of what could happen at any time on the streets.

I saw Hazel had a passenger so we all approached the car with caution. Hazel's fellow traveller was Dot Renwick, the wife of Eric Renwick, another violent gunnie. Eric was a man who suffered no moral discomfort about putting his wife to work on the streets of St Kilda.

It was only when I got closer to the car that I realised there was a third person in the big Ford—a man, lying across the bench seat, his head resting in Hanrahan's lap with his feet eased over Renwick.

Tom opened the passenger door and ordered the two women out of the car. Dot Renwick edged herself out from under the semiconscious man and made her way past me and on to the footpath. 'Get a load of this,' Tom said, gesturing to the inside of the car. 'Now, this is one for the books.'

Peering into the vehicle, I noticed with a start that the man in a drunken stupor wore the black shirt and clerical collar of a priest. The man's trousers and underpants were gathered around his ankles, and his dick was out for all the world to see. An empty sherry bottle had been discarded on the floor of the car.

Hazel Hanrahan's general approach was one of unbridled hostility towards police but as Clarrie opened the driver's side door, she stepped quickly and lightly out of the car. She didn't want to spend the night in the lock-up.

'He's a regular. He lets us drive his car around,' Hazel piped up.

The priest was paralytic. Four years on the beat had prepared me for many of humanity's weaker moments but this was a new low. 'What the bloody hell have I struck tonight?' I thought.

Tom stepped in and shooed the two women away. Hazel and Dot wandered off down the road, cracking their wicked jokes and cackling raucously as they went.

'I'll drive him back to the station,' Jenkins said, pointing to the drunken, semi-naked priest. 'You follow me, Clarrie.'

Clarrie and I arrived back at the station in time to see Tom pull the big Ford into the kerb outside the station. The short drive back seemed to have sobered the priest up a bit. I could see him sitting up in the car, his head bobbing and jerking in silhouette in the passenger seat.

'His name's Father John Day,' Tom told us. 'Reckons he comes from Apollo Bay.'

Tom opened the passenger door and Father John Day of Apollo Bay staggered out of the car. I grabbed Day's arm, helping Tom to walk the priest into the station and sit him down in a chair in the sergeant's office. Day sat swaying in the chair, as drunk as a skunk.

Tom rang St Patrick's Cathedral in East Melbourne and introduced himself. 'We've got one of your priests here—Father John Day from Apollo Bay. We found him in a pretty ordinary state, drunk in his car in the company of prostitutes. I need you to send someone down to pick him up and get his car back here at the station.'

While we waited for the Cathedral to respond, Clarrie and I wandered into the sergeant's room again. I'd never seen a priest in this condition before and I was drawn to him more out of curiosity than anything else.

Day didn't utter a word to me and I couldn't bring myself to speak to him. But I looked at his face intently. He glared back at me with an almost comically pompous look on his face. He did not seem at all worried that he had been detained by police.

Tom yelled out to me to put the billy on, so I turned and left Day to his drunken ruminations.

Within twenty minutes two young priests made their way into the station. They were clearly ill at ease and keen to get Day back to the Cathedral. Clarrie and I stood in the foyer of the station, watching the priests walk gingerly past us. And then we heard Tom give Day the rounds of the kitchen.

'If you are caught in this area again, whether you've got your pants on or not, you will be locked up, Father. Am I making myself clear to you, now?' Jenkins thundered.

The two priests walked Day past us in the foyer, veering from side to side, eager to get him out of the station as quickly as they could.

With Day gone, I took my scheduled break in the lunchroom with Tom and Clarrie. I was bemused by Day's behaviour and bewildered that he'd been released so casually for no other reason than the dog collar he wore around his neck.

'Let's just forget about what happened,' Tom said.

'Why didn't we charge him?' I replied.

'It's a waste of time,' Clarrie chipped in.

'Yep,' Tom said nodding. 'Look, Dinny, I've been around this force long enough to know that we don't charge priests, short of a murder blue.'

I looked at him quizzically and he felt obliged to continue.

'Even if we had charged him, the charges would have been knocked over. It would never get to court,' Tom explained. 'It's best to let him go. Clarrie's right. It would be a bloody waste of time charging that pisspot priest. Just let it go.'

But I could not let it go. If we'd pulled up any old Tom, Dick or Harry drunk, semi-naked and in the company of prostitutes in a car stuttering along the road, he would have been charged. Hazel and Dot had told us that this priest made a habit of visiting prostitutes in Melbourne. Day had been detained but would face no penalty. It troubled me.

Certainly, the image of the drunken priest with his dick out challenged my faith. I'd never seen a priest in that condition before but what bothered me most was that, as police officers, we were discriminating in his favour purely because he was a priest. For days afterwards, the incident gnawed away at me. Finally, I determined to broach the subject again with Tom Jenkins when the right opportunity arose.

Two weeks after we'd pulled Day up, I was on afternoon shift, working with Tom and another constable, Doug Park.

We'd been out on patrol in the van. We pulled back to the station for a break. Doug had made himself scarce, and Tom and I were sitting in the lunchroom having a sandwich. It was time to bring up the Day business again.

'You know that priest we pulled up a couple of weeks back?' I asked.

'The Vatican's finest. Father John Day,' Tom replied.

'Tell me, what's the drill when we lock up a priest?'

'Dinny, we don't lock them up. We let them go. Once you've been around for a while, you'll start to learn that the Catholic Church carries a good deal more clout than the local church on the corner. It's a political organisation. It has wrapped itself around every layer of government. This happens everywhere—all across Australia and probably all over the world, but nowhere does the Catholic Church have more power than it does in the Victoria Police force.'

'So Day can do whatever he likes and he'll never get pulled up for it?'

'Short of a murder blue, he'll walk away every time,' Tom replied.

'This priest is a disgrace. Can't we make a complaint to the Cathedral?'

'Dinny, nothing would happen to Day,' Jenkins answered calmly. 'But if you wanted to make a complaint to the Cathedral, even if you wanted to front Mannix himself, you'd find yourself as lonely as a bastard on Father's Day. This goes all the way to the top. It's not just the police. It's the judges, the lawyers, the politicians.'

Tom took a sip of his tea. He could see that I was troubled by what he had told me.

'Between you and me, I don't agree with it. But there are forces at work here that are stronger than you and me, Dinny. I learnt early on in the job. Don't pick fights you can't win.'

❖

The Victoria Police force ran along the old sectarian fault lines. Tom Jenkins was a Catholic like me. Clarrie Bell was a Protestant and a Freemason. The three of us were a microcosm of the Victoria Police force. We got on well and worked well together, but there was an almost imperceptible divide between Catholic and Protestant.

I'd made my allegiances known back at the police academy. I was in one of the three squads of twenty-five trainees. One morning we were all ordered to fall in for parade. A superintendent and two inspectors were present, watching over us.

Our drill instructor was First Constable Allen Coombes. He'd been a lieutenant colonel in the army and had seen action in Crete and Bougainville. He'd been awarded the Military Cross. After Crete he'd helped train the Second AIF in jungle warfare at Atherton in Queensland before they headed off to fight the Japanese in New Guinea. He was a powerfully built and imposing man. All the trainees were quietly terrified of him.

Coombes ordered us at ease and in his gravelly, stern voice ordered us to attend the St Paul's Anglican Cathedral for the annual police service on the following Sunday.

I wasn't an Anglican and I wasn't going to go to an Anglican service. I came to attention. I took one step forward and one to the right and stamped my feet hard on the bitumen of the parade ground.

'Sir!' I screamed out.

'Yes, Ryan. What is your complaint?' Coombes barked.

'Sir, I am a Catholic and I am forbidden by my faith to enter another church.'

Coombes, mouth agape for a moment, was stunned by my temerity.

'Then you are excused on religious grounds,' Coombes said, his brow furrowed.

With that, another trainee, Tom Atkinson, a young bloke from Warrnambool, stepped forward and meekly announced that he was a Catholic, too.

Coombes excused Tom from attending the Anglican service. He waited to see if there were any more hellions demanding religious freedom but there were none, and the parade was dismissed shortly afterwards.

I didn't realise what a stir this had caused at the time. My religion was important to me. I may have been young and impulsive but all I thought I was doing was following the directions of the Church. I had no idea that my challenge to Coombes would filter through the police force in a brush fire of whispers and religious espionage that was the main game in the Victoria Police force at the time.

Within the force the Masons had their spies and the Catholics had theirs. I was marked as one of 'them' by the Freemasons and as one of 'us' by the Catholics. I didn't have a clue about any of this at the time. I was still a trainee, not yet sworn in as a police officer. But that's how the system worked. The Freemasons looked after their own and the Catholics looked after theirs.

The story of my audacious interruption of Allen Coombes would precede me wherever I went as a uniformed officer.

I don't know that it advanced my career in any way, nor do I think that it held me back, but from the moment I challenged Coombes on the parade ground, the Catholics within the force saw me as one of them.

Not long after I finished my training and took my oath as a police officer, I was stationed at Russell Street. Every constable coming out of the academy was sent to Russell Street at first. I was doing foot and bicycle patrols in the CBD, patrolling the grounds at Parliament House and occasionally keeping an eye on the corpses down at the morgue.

I was boarding above Russell Street headquarters. The top floors of the building were devoted to accommodation for single policemen. I was on the ninth floor and Bob Saker had his room across the hallway.

Bob and I got on very well. Like me, he loved his cricket. We played together for the Russell Street XI, and I'd roomed with him at the academy. On the day I had stepped forward and told Allen Coombes that I could not enter an Anglican church, Bob was standing alongside me. He had no problem with going to St Paul's. He was an Anglican.

As young uniform policemen we were both drawn to the 'Shadowers'—the Observation Squad. Fresh out of the academy, Bob and I played cricket with a lot of them. There were VIPs to guard and protect. Crims to watch over, disguises to be worn, shadows to lurk in. It seemed to Bob and me that it was a very exciting line of police work.

I'd heard on the grapevine that the Shadowers was full of Masons. They were under the charge of Detective Senior Sergeant Gil Brown, who was described to me by my cricket mates as 'a narrow-minded bigot and a staunch Mason'.

I didn't quite know what to make of it. But if my cricket mates were anything to go by, the Masons ruled the roost in the Shadowers.

I asked Bob if he was a Mason. Maybe he would have a leg up in the Shadowers that way.

'No, mate,' Bob told me. 'I'm not a Mason.'

Bob was about my size and shape. Sometimes he'd come into my room and grab a shirt of mine to wear to spare himself doing his laundry. He didn't have to ask. We were good mates. He'd help himself.

One night I was in my room, about to go out. I looked for my best shirt and found it was missing. It could only be in Bob's room so I crossed over the corridor to get it back.

I looked into his cupboard and checked the bottom first because that was where I expected to find it. There it was, along with Bob's Masonic apron and the rest of the regalia.

When next I saw Bob, I couldn't let it pass: 'Bob, I went and got my shirt back out of your room. You *are* a Mason. I saw your apron in the cupboard.'

He blushed and stammered a bit before acknowledging it. He was clearly embarrassed.

'You've got nothing to be ashamed of,' I told him. 'I hear it's a pretty good organisation. You might even get into the Shadowers before me.'

I didn't care if my fellow police officers were Hindus or Buddhists or genuflected to goats. It didn't bother me at all. I had my faith and that was my business, and what Bob or anyone else did was theirs.

I had mates in the police force from all backgrounds and I never prejudged them. Certainly, I did gravitate towards other Catholics in the force, usually over a beer, but not to the exclusion of other police who may have popped on an apron every Wednesday night. That was the way it was. Those who became Masons did so thinking they might get a boost through the force, while the Catholics gravitated towards their Catholic senior officers in the force. It happened almost unconsciously. It was a natural consequence of sectarianism in Australian society at the time.

For a young uniform copper not long out of the academy, the Catholic–Mason divide operated almost invisibly. I did not know that dark forces existed within these groups and that they were answering to authorities outside the police force.

But I had my first view of it when the drunken pervert, Father John Day, stumbled out of St Kilda police station without charge. I did not like what I had seen.

2

DITCHING THE UNIFORM

But who shall guard the guardians?
JUVENAL, LATE 1ST CENTURY—EARLY 2ND CENTURY

I didn't like thugs and crooks. I resented them. I hated thieves especially, and I detested bullies of any stripe. I wanted to be at the sharp end of policing. I wanted to be a detective. Perhaps it was in my genes.

There was nothing wrong with uniform work. I had been in uniform for four years. I'd loved it—even when I was working traffic at St Kilda Junction, where seven of Melbourne's biggest streets merged into one, with trams, cars and trucks and me as the sole arbiter of who would progress and who'd have to stay put. People hanging their feet out of the tram would inadvertently give me a kick or two as they went past.

The way the junction sank in the middle, I must have looked like Toulouse Lautrec to all the people passing by. And my work did not go unnoticed. The Melbourne *Sun* gave me a mention: 'Congratulations to the young constable working the traffic beat at the St Kilda Junction. It's a tough job and he does it well but we suggest that he buy himself a butter box to stand on so he can be seen by the passing traffic.'

It was often cold, and when it rained I'd be standing in puddles. Even then I enjoyed it.

But my real desire was to be a detective in the force. I passed the detectives' exam—came third in the class and ditched the uniform in 1956.

Over the next six months, I was at Russell Street headquarters, attached to the Larceny and General Squad, the Observation Squad, the Larceny from Motor Vehicles Squad and the Breaking Squad. I worked at Frankston CIB for three months, filling in for a detective who'd copped a nasty injury. And when a vacancy came up in Mordialloc, just around the corner from my home, I applied for it and got it.

I had my fair share of rough and tumble experiences, like most detectives. In 1957 I was at Russell Street as a detective senior constable, attached to the Breakers. I was out on patrol with Mick Murphy, who was the same rank—a pair of new detectives in our new suits.

We were driving around East Melbourne, along Gipps Street, in the CIB car, a Twin Spinner Ford. It was just after midnight. We saw a Ford Prefect parked outside a block of flats and the silhouette of a man perched at the steering wheel. Mick knocked on the window and announced us. The driver reluctantly opened the door and got out. He was a big lump of a bloke. A Collingwood six-footer, built like a brick shithouse, in his mid-thirties by my reckoning. He handed over his licence. His name was Harry Clifford Gribbin. He seemed affronted that we had pulled him out of his car. When I asked him what he was doing, he scowled.

'What's it got to do with you?'

We searched his car and found a loaded single-shot rifle, with a bullet in the chamber, alongside the base of the front seat. We opened the boot and found it was full to the brim with plastic raincoats. Gribbin couldn't provide any reasonable explanation for the presence of raincoats in his boot. There was the usual blabber about getting them from a friend he'd met in a pub, a friend he was unable to name.

We arrested him for unlawful possession. Oddly, Gribbin seemed to calm down after we arrested him.

But Mick and I had a logistical problem to deal with—how to get both cars back to Russell Street. Mick explained to Gribbin that we could handcuff him and take him back to Russell Street in the CIB car, then either Mick or I would come back and pick up Gribbin's car. Or, if Gribbin was going to behave himself, I could sit alongside him while he drove his Ford Prefect to Russell Street and Mick would follow, driving in the Twin Spinner. Suddenly, Gribbin became a shining light of helpfulness and co-operation.

'I've got nothing to worry about. We can sort all of this out back at Russell Street,' he said, making his way back to his car.

Gribbin took the wheel of the Ford Prefect with me riding shotgun. I felt in control of the situation. I was armed with my .32 Colt service pistol in my shoulder holster and my handcuffs over my belt. I wasn't expecting any trouble.

That was a mistake.

The sly mongrel took off slowly enough but when he got on to Hoddle Street, he hit the accelerator hard. The little Ford Prefect had a top speed of about eighty kilometres an hour, a good metre or two slower than Mick's Twin Spinner, but Gribbin started swerving in and out of traffic and quickly left Mick in his wake.

When Gribbin failed to make the right-hand turn and proceeded along on the wrong side of Punt Road, I realised that his co-operation had come to an end.

'Harry,' I told him, 'don't be bloody silly.'

Gribbin didn't say a word. He had a look of grim determination on his face as he kept dodging oncoming traffic. I was armed to the teeth, but I couldn't do a thing about it. I sat there in the passenger seat in a state of grace, too nervous to move and praying Gribbin's desperate dash would soon come to an end.

He swerved hard into Swan Street, Richmond, then right into a side street. He pushed the little car down the street another 100 metres or so then slammed the brakes on, thrusting the narrow little car to a sharp halt on the kerb.

The car rattled to and fro with the impact and we rattled along with it.

Once the car finally came to rest, Gribbin jumped out. I took off after him and brought him down with a tackle that would have put Dally Messenger to shame. But rather than sliding along on the hallowed turf of the SCG, I found myself crashing onto the bluestones of Richmond and coming up covered with the detritus of the inner city gutter all over my suit.

Gribbin and I punched on in the gutter, the city slime caking us both. I felt obliged to resort to foul play. I pulled my handcuffs off my belt and gave Gribbin a couple of hard smacks to the head, swinging the cuffs and chain like a mace.

It didn't deter him much. We continued to sprawl about in the gutter until I heard what I took to be the voice of the Archangel Gabriel booming: 'What's going on here?'

I looked up at a large uniform police officer on foot patrol.

'I'm a police officer!' I yelled out, eager to prevent him laying into me, too. My large, blue-shirted new friend came to my assistance and commenced the process of disentangling me from Gribbin.

Finally, Mick arrived in the CIB car. I was out of the shit. Harry Gribbin, however, was in plenty.

Gribbin was charged with a string of offences, including larceny of the goods we'd found in the boot of his car, resisting arrest, assaulting police and firearms offences. The judge took a dim view of his activities and sentenced him to a long stretch.

About the only thing he wasn't charged with was kidnapping. That didn't stop my fellow police officers back at Russell Street bestowing on me the title of the 'Last copper kidnapped since Ned Kelly was about'. Laughter all round.

All I cared about was that the dry-cleaners gave my new—now soiled and shit-stained—suit their very best attention.

That was what it was like being a detective. Each day was different to the last, and any time you signed on for a shift, there was no way of knowing what surprises were in store.

❖

Sooner or later, a police detective in Victoria would be offered a bribe. It was a natural action for crims to offer a police officer a quid to look the other way.

I got a serious offer one day in 1960. Detective Sergeant Jack Meehan and I were investigating thefts from building sites around Melbourne. About £15,000 (equivalent to almost $400,000 today) worth of gear—stoves, hot-water systems, window frames, sinks, baths, even the toilets had been stolen from a block of ten Glen Iris flats that were a day or two away from being finished and sold off.

Jack was a World War II veteran who had seen active duty in New Guinea. He had played a few games for St Kilda and sported the number two guernsey for the club. He was a tough man and as honest as the day is long.

Jack and I received some information that a breaker, James Kelly, was responsible for the building site thefts. Kelly had a criminal record longer than my arm and his put together. When Jack and I paid Kelly a visit, he had a heap of stolen property at his house. He eventually coughed to the break, enter and steals.

He was more than forthcoming because he felt that he'd been cheated by 'Fishy' Taylor, a known fence who operated out of a junkyard in Richmond. Out of the £15,000 worth of gear Kelly had lifted, Fishy had flicked him only £3000. Kelly told us we could expect to find most of the gear still on Fishy's premises.

And so it transpired. Sinks, baths, stoves and a whole lot of other stolen gear were stored in Fishy's lock-up. There was so much stolen gear that the police van had to make five trips back and forth to the police academy, where it was stored as evidence.

When we walked into Fishy's cluttered little office, he knew we had him cold. He seemed resigned to his fate.

He got up and opened the safe behind them. There were thousands of pounds in nice, neat tidy piles.

'That's yours,' Fishy said, motioning at Jack and me.

'Stick it up your arse, Fishy,' Jack replied. 'Dinny and I aren't interested.'

Fishy shrugged. 'If you don't take it, someone else will.'

We took him back to St Kilda police station and charged him with receiving stolen property.

The next time I saw Fishy we were both in court. He was in the dock and I was giving evidence against him. Jack Meehan was the police prosecutor. We had a big team there. We expected that the magistrate would view proceedings as a committal and refer the matter for judgment in a higher court.

Fishy put his hand up and pleaded guilty, and the magistrate determined that the matter would go no further. He looked solemnly at Fishy and handed down his sentence. Jack and I expected him to get five years. The magistrate thought otherwise and gave Fishy a twelve-month good behaviour bond.

Fishy walked past us on his way out the door.

'I told you someone else would trouser it,' he said, with a smirk on his face.

❖

As detectives we worked hard and often investigated the lowest forms of human conduct. There were no counsellors to help us through some of the ugly and grim crimes we witnessed. More often than not our counselling sessions took place in pubs where we'd drink ourselves to oblivion, shake the cobwebs out the next day and be back at work on time, every time.

It was that way for many who worked in the criminal justice system. I remember drinking at the Celtic Club until the wee hours on a number of occasions. If you'd scanned the crowded bar there you would have found judges, lawyers and other coppers all on the sauce. There was a certain recklessness to it that made me believe that they, like me, were drinking to forget.

When I transferred to Mordialloc in 1958, the CIB branch—me, Detective Senior Constable Milton 'Mitch' Mitchell and Detective Sergeant Ray Child—made a habit of going to the local RSL. It was six o'clock closing in Victoria back then, and we knew that if we ever knocked off late, we could always get a beer at the local RSL.

The six o'clock closing law was stupidity itself. It was Australia's version of the *Volstead Act*. The United States had prohibition but in Australia we had the six o'clock swill to appease the temperance societies and wowsers. Unlike prohibition in the States, which ended in 1933, six o'clock closing remained in place for fifty years in Victoria until 1966.

We always paid for our grog but the president was happy to keep the taps on for us. We weren't the only ones in there having a surreptitious beer or three. Other members of the club enjoyed the hospitality, too, despite the fact that the club was unlicensed after six o'clock.

I got to know the president of the club pretty well. He was a leading figure in the local area, and was well respected. He'd held officer's rank in the army in World War II.

One of the members of the club told me he had heard that the president was 'having it on' with a particular boy in the community. The boy was known to locals as being 'a bit slow'. I spoke to the boy's parents to gain their trust then arranged an interview with the young lad. I discovered he had a mild intellectual disability. He had difficulty gathering and articulating his thoughts, but after an exhausting interview for both of us, the boy provided me with a lengthy statement, detailing anal rape and a myriad of other sexual offences he had suffered over many years at the hands of the president of Mordialloc RSL.

I interviewed the president who, after he was presented with the evidence against him, confessed to his crimes. He was charged and went before the courts. Despite glowing references from other stalwarts of the community, he received a six-year jail sentence.

Around the same time, Mitch and I investigated a complaint that had been made against the Methodist minister at Cheltenham. The minister was also a scout leader in the area. The complaint was that he had performed bizarre rituals on young boys initiated into the scouts. The scouts would be stripped off, covered in oil and tied to a post in the scout hall. The minister would then proceed to assault and rape the young boys.

Mitch and I interviewed him. It was Mitch's case and I assisted. The minister was charged with a raft of child sex offences, including buggery and gross indecency. He pleaded guilty and was sentenced to thirteen years in prison.

I presumed every police officer in Victoria held the same view of child sex offences. I would learn that I was wrong.

❖

There is a myth in Australian society today that sex offences against children were rarely, if ever, pursued by police. My own experiences debunk that. When information came forward, police pursued crimes against children with purpose.

In my time as a police officer and detective, I charged many men with sexual crimes against children, from snow dropping—the theft of girls' underwear from backyard clothes lines—all the way to rape and buggery, as did all the detectives I knew.

These crimes scandalised even hardened police officers. They certainly shocked me, but no matter how appalling the crimes were and how revolted we may have felt, I would not be deterred from pursuing the perpetrators, no matter who they were or what status they enjoyed in the community.

I wasn't evangelistic about it. I just saw it as my duty.

The Mordialloc RSL president was a military officer and a combat veteran, but the high esteem the community held him in afforded him no protection from the dispensation of justice.

The Methodist minister represented a religious organisation that had hundreds of thousands of followers across Australia, some of them in the police force, others in positions of authority. Yet he, too, felt the full force of the law when his crimes against children came to the attention of police.

❖

Fred Russell was a detective sergeant in the early 1960s. He would go on to be the head of the CIB in Victoria in the late 1970s. He was a suave man, tall and powerfully built, with a head of thick brown hair that he kept slicked back and parted neatly on the left. He had the air of a Hollywood actor.

Fred and I had played cricket together with the Russell Street side. I kept wickets and Fred bowled more than handy medium pace. I used to annoy him by coming up to the stumps when he bowled. Like all medium pace bowlers, Fred thought he was a yard or two quicker than he was.

He was of more senior rank than me but, with our shared experiences on the cricket field, we regarded each other as friends. He also knew, as other senior coppers who were Catholics knew, that I was a Catholic, too.

The Hotel Spencer, in West Melbourne, was one of our haunts. It was a ramshackle tavern that provided a basic meal and a beer to travellers and a select group of CIB detectives—ninety-nine per cent of whom were Catholics. We never referred to the pub by its name. To us, it was O'Connor's—named after its amiable publican who, being Irish and Catholic, liked a drink more than most. Some of my colleagues referred to the pub as 'the Green Door', an obtuse reference to its Irish Catholic clientele.

Leo O'Connor was a good publican. Despite the number of beers he poured into himself on a regular basis, he always maintained his good humour.

The place would be fit to burst on St Patrick's Day.

One afternoon I was part of a group of detectives enjoying a beer at O'Connor's. To this day I'm not sure why, because I was a junior detective of lowly rank, but I seemed to get on well with more senior detectives. I'd often have a drink with others higher up the ladder. I was standing around with a glass in hand with Detective Sergeant Jack Hague, Detective Inspector Frank Holland, Detective Chief Inspector Kevin Carton and Detective Chief Inspector Bill Mooney. And Detective Sergeant Fred Russell was making up the shout.

Fred pulled me aside in between beers. He and I wandered to a dark corner of the pub before he stopped and scanned the room.

'Look, Dinny, what I'm about to tell you is in the strictest confidence.'

I nodded my consent.

'I don't know if you know this but there is a group of us who, at the request of the Cathedral, look into instances where priests have been charged with offences to see if we can have these matters dropped or dismissed so the Church's good name will not be brought into disrepute.'

Fred paused and looked at me intently before continuing with his spiel. 'We know your strong belief. We'd like to invite you to join us. You should give this some consideration and let me know as soon as you can.'

No names were mentioned, but it was clear that the requests had come from the highest echelons of the Catholic Church in Melbourne.

I thought of Tommy Jenkins's warning after we'd dragged Day back to the station three years earlier: 'There's no point in charging the priest, Dinny,' Jenkins had said then. 'We'd be ostracised by the Catholics within the force if we tried to charge him.'

And here I was at O'Connor's presented with one of the faces that would have knocked the charges over and sent me to Coventry to boot. It was obvious to me that Fred Russell and this group were engaging in multiple conspiracies to pervert the course of justice.

I did not appreciate the extent of it at the time. I presumed the group that Fred had asked me to join was involved in relatively minor matters—misdemeanours, traffic offences, drink driving and so forth. The sorts of crimes that were of no profound criminality but would necessarily bring embarrassment to the Church. I didn't like it and I didn't want a bar of it, but I had no idea that this conspiracy would include protecting paedophile priests.

Nevertheless, I was genuinely taken aback. I stumbled out an awkward reply, saying I'd get back to him in a couple of days.

I met up with Fred a couple of days later and told him I wasn't interested in joining this shadowy group. He took my rejection in a matter of fact way. He certainly didn't seem put out.

'Oh, well,' he said. 'Fair enough. It's your decision.'

Fred Russell was an intelligent and astute fellow. But he did have a dark chamber tucked away in the corner of his soul that forced him to completely lose his way as a policeman. His allegiance to the Catholic Church trespassed deeply into the bounds of his duties.

He had not told me who else was in this group. I did not know who they might have been but they, like Fred, took their orders, in part at least, from St Patrick's Cathedral. These men suffered from a distorted sense of loyalty to the Church. And that misguided loyalty drove them to ignore their oath to the police force and to the people of Victoria they purported to serve.

For its part, the Church unashamedly corrupted these men in the pursuit of its own interests.

Catholics made up about half the Victoria Police force. For the overwhelming majority of police officers in Victoria, religion and the performance of their duties were never in conflict. But at the extremes, there were the Protestants who had entered the secretive and clannish world of Freemasonry who advanced their own, and the Catholics like Fred Russell who did likewise.

I continued to practise my faith. I went to mass every Sunday at St Brigid's in Mordialloc. The parish priest there was Father Jim. He was Irish born and carried the strong brogue of the Emerald Isle. He wasn't a drinker but he smoked like a chimney, often extinguishing one cigarette and lighting another in one effortless movement. He was a decent man, a good priest with a boisterous sense of humour.

'It doesn't matter if you're a Catholic or a Protestant,' Father Jim would often pronounce. 'Just as long as you're Irish.'

One day he invited me up to the presbytery for a cup of coffee. We had met up there on many occasions. We often sat and sipped coffee and discussed how I was getting on in the police force and the Church in general.

I had expected nothing more than just another convivial chat, but in the middle of our conversation, Father Jim trailed off, paused and leaned forward in his chair. He looked at me with an earnestness that I had never seen on his face before.

'Do you know that a priest was caught by the police down at Chelsea Beach exposing himself to young girls?'

He paused again.

'Somehow this priest was not charged. Dinny, if something similar arises in the course of your duties, I want you to charge the offending priest. These things must stop.'

I thought, 'Shit, another one.' My mind went back to Day in the front seat of his car. And then back to the corner of the bar at O'Connor's where Fred Russell had spoken to me in whispers about joining the clandestine group. It seemed like Fred Russell's group had been at work. I don't know if Fred was involved. There's no reason to believe he may have been, but I was able to do the basic arithmetic.

It was just as Tom Jenkins had told me after we grabbed Day—there was nothing I could do about it. I just kept my head down and got on with my work. I loved the police force. I enjoyed locking up crooks.

❖

I lived with my young family in Aspendale, a bayside suburb on the southern fringes of Melbourne, closer to the southern extremities of the city at Frankston than to the Melbourne CBD. Our home, a modest three-bedroom weatherboard in a cul-de-sac, was a kilometre or so from Mordialloc police station. More often than not, I would walk to work. We didn't own a car. We didn't have a phone. We had a close connection with our neighbours, who were happy to have a police officer living in the street.

I'd often work a sixty-hour week. This left Jean with most of the work to do at home, raising and caring for the children. She took it all in her stride. She was a perfect policeman's wife. Even if I got home full after a night on the tiles, there was never a harsh word between us. She understood that I had to let off a bit of steam from time to time.

The house was less than a kilometre from the beach and, in Melbourne's cool winters, in particular, the westerlies would whip off the water and cast a big chill over the suburb. Our three children—Michael, 6, Martin, 3, and Gavin, 2—were kept rugged up in the winter months.

One night in early February 1962, Jean and I were woken by the sound of Michael's laboured breathing. We raced into his bedroom to see him going blue in the face. I immediately thought it was an asthma attack. Michael had no history of asthma but somehow I knew what the problem was. Jean stayed with him while I threw on a few clothes and dashed off to the public phone box outside the Aspendale shops, about 500 metres away.

I rang the family doctor, De Coursey Shaw. By the time I got home he had arrived at the house. Shaw was in his dressing gown, having dashed out of his house as quickly as he could.

We both went inside. Michael was lying on his side while Jean gently stroked his hair. Michael's face was a deathly grey. He did not appear to be breathing.

Shaw told Jean and me to get Michael to sit up. I held Michael with my right hand on his back, propping him up. The doctor went to his medical bag and pulled out a syringe with a very long needle.

Within seconds Shaw was ready and moved quickly over to Michael. The needle punctured the top of Michael's shoulder and Shaw slowly pushed it down, searching for his heart. Satisfied that he had found it, he pushed down on the plunger, sending a dose of adrenaline into Michael's heart. Within seconds, Michael's colour returned and he began to breathe. Shaw told me to keep Michael sitting up for several minutes. He began breathing normally.

The doctor stayed for an hour or more before leaving, declaring Michael was on the improve.

Jean and I stayed up most of the night, taking it in turns to grab a few minutes sleep here and there. We were both emotionally drained from the experience. Jean wept openly in the kitchen, and I held and comforted her.

Shaw returned the following morning. He told Jean and me that Michael had made a full recovery but the asthma attack could be the first of many, and that one day an attack might prove fatal. Little was known about asthma, Shaw told us. There were no medications to treat it beyond a few old wives' remedies. About the only thing he could recommend was that Michael would be better off in a dry, warm climate. The cold winters at Aspendale were doing Michael no good. We would have to move.

After Shaw left, I rang Ray Child and told him what had happened. He told me to take the day off, then come in and see him the following day. It left me a day to think.

I'd spent three months in Brisbane two years before, sent up there on what was known as interchange, where detectives would swap and work in different jurisdictions. I'd worked with the Consorting Squad up in Queensland, often working the racetracks at Doomben, Eagle Farm and Beaudesert. A lot of Victorian crooks travelled to Queensland for a break or to get their noses into trouble north of the Tweed. I enjoyed my time there. I liked Brisbane and the local police looked after me very well.

A month or so before Michael's asthma attack, I'd been seconded to work with a young officer from the Commonwealth police. At the time, the Commonwealth police was headed by Victorian detective, Ernie 'The Harp' Craig. The young Commonwealth copper told me that The Harp was looking for Victorian detectives to recruit for what would become the Australian Federal Police. Victorian detectives were sought after because they were trained in a dedicated school that didn't exist elsewhere in Australia. The young officer asked if I was interested. I was pretty happy where I was, so I knocked him back.

'Are you sure, mate? If you sign on, you'll be promoted straight away to detective sergeant.'

I told him I'd think about it but I really wasn't keen.

On the strength of that exchange, I'd received a call from one of The Harp's underlings, who told me there was a position in Brisbane if I wanted it. I declined the offer but my son's asthma forced me to reconsider it.

By the time I saw Ray the following day, I'd almost made up my mind to go to Brisbane. I told Ray that I was thinking of moving on. He got straight on the phone to Alfie Carruthers, the CIB detective inspector for the area.

Alfie told Ray that he'd speak to Hugh Clugston, a superintendent and boss of the CIB. The wheels were in motion. Within a couple of hours, Hugh got back to me and told me that a vacancy was coming up in Mildura. The job was mine if I wanted it.

'Stay with us, Dinny. Don't go moving interstate,' Clugston told me.

The job of CIB detective in Mildura was listed in *Police Orders*, a weekly newsletter that listed all the promotions, vacancies and appointments. I decided to go for it. Within a fortnight, I had the job and was on my way to Mildura with my family.

Jean was apprehensive about leaving Melbourne. She'd grown up in Melbourne and lived there all her life. Her mother and sister were there. She didn't want to leave.

Neither of us had been to Mildura. It was as far as you could go in Victoria without leaving the state—an outpost of the force and a vast region which bordered New South Wales and South Australia to oversee.

I didn't want to leave either. I was grateful to be staying in the Victoria Police force but I was a city detective. It was my environment. The transfer also meant that any prospect of promotion had ceased.

Both Jean and I were worried about the level of health care that would be available in Mildura to Michael, in particular. We wondered about the schools in the town and whether all the boys would have access to a good education. This was going to be a big move, life-changing for all of us, and once we'd made our way up there, there would be no turning back.

As a detective in Mildura, I was required to provide my own car. I'd receive a vehicle allowance, which was fine, but at that stage I didn't own a car. I put myself in debt to the Police Credit Union and went out and bought an EK standard Holden sedan. I thought I was it and a bit more in my new car.

I rented the house in Aspendale to a friend and his family. It was really my one remaining physical connection with Melbourne.

But Jean and I were determined to make a go of it. Michael's health depended on us living in Mildura and we had no other options.

The morning after my appointment to the Mildura CIB appeared in the *Police Orders*, I got a phone call at the CIB office at Mordialloc. It was Detective Sergeant Dinny Barritt, a good friend of mine. We'd played cricket together in the Russell Street side. He wasn't a great cricketer but he enjoyed the game and loved being part of the team.

'I see you're in the *Police Orders* today for the position at Mildura CIB,' Dinny Barritt said.

'That's right, Dinny,' I replied.

'I'm extremely worried about you going up there,' Dinny told me.

'Why's that?' I inquired, with a sinking feeling rumbling away in my guts.

'My brother Jim, who you know is in charge of the CIB in Mildura. You definitely will not get on well with him because there's something really wrong with him in the head.'

'What are you getting at?' I asked.

'Look, why don't you come in to the police club and we'll have a beer. I'll tell you all about it.'

I was more than curious. I was worried. After making the decision to throw the family into tumult, the last thing I wanted to hear was that I was headed into a nightmare. Dinny was keen to fill me in on the details sooner rather than later, so we agreed to meet later that day.

DITCHING THE UNIFORM

The Police Association Club was in MacKenzie Street, right alongside Russell Street headquarters. I got there around five o'clock and Dinny was there waiting for me. He bought me a beer. I took a sip and cleared my throat.

'So what's the problem with your brother?'

'Jim has set ideas of his own which I disagree with, as do most other policemen who know him,' Dinny told me, with a look of anguish on his face.

'What do you mean?' I asked. I thought Dinny was being obtuse. I needed some details. 'In what way?'

'I know you to a degree but I know Jim much better,' He said. 'I'm telling you now for certain that you will not get on with him. Don't go up there.'

I took my time to explain to him that the only reason I was going to Mildura was for the health of my eldest son. It was something I had to do.

'All I can do is repeat what I have already told you,' he said seriously. 'Don't go to Mildura.'

'My hands are tied, Dinny,' I replied. 'There's nothing I can do about this.'

'All right,' he said and downed his beer. 'I'm sorry I couldn't convince you. Don't forget—I did warn you.'

I finished my beer and made my way home. I caught the train from Flinders Street back to Mordialloc, and as the old red carriage swayed and creaked down the line, I thought about what I might be getting myself into.

My mind went back to an annual police mass at St Francis in Lonsdale Street two years earlier. Afterwards, a group of us crossed the road and went to Myer's for breakfast. After breakfast, some of us took a stroll down Lonsdale Street to

O'Connor's in Spencer Street. I was walking along with Dinny Barritt and his brother Barney. Barney was a detective sergeant who'd worked down in Geelong for most of his career.

We were having a normal chat about police gossip, with a few funny stories thrown in for good measure. Barney looked back at the coppers walking behind us to the pub.

'The bastard's behind us,' Barney said to his brother. 'It's your turn. I had to put up with him last year.'

Dinny made it clear he didn't want the bastard either.

'Come on, Barney. Let's see what we can do to work this out.'

I looked back and saw this fellow. He was a giant of a man, built like a front rower with a head the size of a watermelon. I quickly gathered from their conversation that the large bloke they were each trying to offload was their older brother, Jim. I reckoned the Barritts' domestic disputes were their business and not mine, so I hurried on and joined up with another group a few metres ahead.

That was the only time I'd ever seen Jim Barritt. I'd heard about him. I knew he'd been stationed at Footscray, where he'd developed a reputation for being very hard on the slaughtermen who worked in the abattoirs around there. He used to beat the shit out of them, or so I'd heard.

Another little glimmer of memory came to me.

Back in 1957 when I was relieving at Frankston CIB, my boss, Detective Sergeant Len Walsh, and I were having a beer at the Chelsea Hotel. A bloke came up to us; Len knew him and introduced me to him. It was Lloyd Brewster, a violent standover man who ran some of the big baccarat schools around Melbourne. Brewster was whingeing to Len about policemen in general, about how we were all cowards and would only go the thump when we knew we were safe.

'The only copper with any guts that I know is Jim Barritt,' Brewster said. 'He didn't wait for the doors to open at the baccarat school. He'd go straight through them.'

Did Jim Barritt rule the Mildura district like his own personal fiefdom? Was he corrupt? Was he a violent bastard who threw the standing orders away? Was he sane? How the hell was I going to get on with him?

I decided then that I was going to go out of my way to work with this man. There were very few policemen I'd met whom I couldn't get along with. In general I had no problem working with any other police officer in Victoria.

As they say, 'All the world is a little queer other than thee and me, and even thee art a little queer.'

Besides, Jim Barritt couldn't be that bad, could he?

3

THE DEEP NORTH

Once I cried: 'Oh, God Almighty!
if Thy might doth still endure,
Now show me in a vision for the wrongs of Earth a cure.'
HENRY LAWSON, 1867–1922

I knew little about Mildura before I got there in 1962. What I did know was that Jean and the children and I were headed to a far-flung township in the north-west corner of Victoria.

The heat bore down on us throughout the journey. It was a stifling day as we motored along in my new car, with the mercury hovering around 35 degrees Celsius, the boot laden with our prize possessions and clothing. A van with our furniture was awaiting our arrival in Mildura. When I'd bought the car, I'd considered air conditioning a luxury I could not afford, a decision I would desperately regret as the temperature in the car climbed higher the further north we drove.

Even in the heat, Martin, Michael and Gavin chattered away excitedly throughout the trip, pausing only to take in a landmark here and there before resuming their enthusiastic conversation. They saw our move to Mildura as an adventure. Children have no fear of the new, only curiosity.

But Jean and I remained anxious. We sat quietly in the front seat as I drove, taking in the shape of the landscape as it changed from the grassy pastures around Bendigo to become flatter and dryer, the land now shifting to broad-acre farming—sheep and wheat—until we hit Sea Lake and the Mallee.

The children's chatter ceased as they peered through the open windows at a scene that was unknown to all of us—strange and forbidding. On either side of the road lay flat scrub, pockmarked with the famed mallee gums, their limbs reaching out crazily in all directions, eking out an existence among the salt bush in the dusty pink soil. Every living thing there seemed overpowered, dominated by the shimmering heat.

I looked across at Jean. She was crying, her head bowed, sobbing into her handkerchief. The Mallee, named by someone with a sense of humour as 'the Sunset Country', was a bleak and tormented place, and the sense of remoteness and isolation hung heavily in the air. We were just six hours' drive from Melbourne but we might as well have been on the other side of the planet. I drove on, wondering what I had done and how my family would deal with the challenges of living in Mildura.

Twenty kilometres out of Mildura, the landscape changed again, the bleak semi-desert transformed into farms with their neat rows of grape vines, a sign of the area's dried fruit industry.

The irrigation channels around Red Cliffs, a satellite township of Mildura, had been open since the 1920s, creating an inland oasis wedged between the cartographers' lines on the map and separating Victoria, South Australia and the Murray River to the north and into New South Wales. In Red Cliffs and then in Mildura, neat, uniform little houses lined the streets with their lush and green front lawns, trimmed to precision, while the sprinklers hissed and clanged, their fine mists spreading life to the thirsty gardens.

The greater Mildura area appeared to be bigger than its then population of 27,000 people. There was an air of productivity, of success against the odds. It was March and the picking season was under way, the town swelling with itinerant labourers, many of whom arrived from Melbourne on trains to torture their bodies in the orchards and piss their wages up against a wall in one of the two hotels in the town.

Jean was troubled and I knew immediately that she felt the sense of distance from home, family and friends. With the warnings about Jim Barritt still ringing in my ears, I determined that I would make a go of Mildura for Jean and the children, even if it meant befriending the devil himself.

❖

Just one day into the job at Mildura and I knew what Dinny Barritt was talking about.

Jim Barritt wanted to give me the guided tour. The first stop on the way was a meet and greet with the local parish priest. I thought this was strange but any protest was out of the question. I went along for the ride.

Barritt and I arrived at the presbytery. And who did he introduce me to? None other than Father John Day. I knew at once that he was the drunken, lecherous priest I had encountered six years before. He might have been as pissed as a newt back then, but he remembered me too. I could see the glimmer of recognition in his eyes; his body language was immediately defensive.

I didn't say a word at the time but on the drive back to the station with Barritt, I decided to speak up. 'You know that priest has got some unusual habits,' I said.

Barritt swung around. 'What do you mean by that?'

I told Barritt about detaining Day in Melbourne—the prostitutes, and Day lying there on the front seat of the car with his head in a prostitute's lap and his dick hanging out.

'You don't know what you're talking about!' Barritt roared. 'Get your facts right before you open your gob.'

Barritt may have been the senior officer, but I never took a backward step when I knew I was right. I was surprised at his reaction and I was not about to be bullied. 'I've got my facts right. It's you that needs to get your facts right.'

After that, the guided tour was over. We travelled back to the station in silence.

We had similar exchanges throughout the day. He would approach me and yell at me from less than a foot away and I would return the favour.

At the station the following day, Barritt yelled out that I was wanted on the phone. I picked up the phone at my desk and introduced myself.

'It's Father Day, Denis. I'd like you to come over to the presbytery now, if you could.'

I had an inkling that Barritt had told Day what I had said. Curious, I jumped in the car and headed straight over. I knocked on the presbytery door, and it opened almost immediately. Day had been waiting. He launched right into me.

'You need to get your facts straight. You don't know what you're talking about. That wasn't me. There was another priest named John Day. He was down at Apollo Bay. I've never been to the place.'

I adjusted my volume to equal his. 'It was you. You and I both know it was you in the company of prostitutes and in a disgraceful condition.'

His voice rose another few decibels. 'Get out of my sight. Don't you spread malicious rumours about me. Get out.'

Too late. I'd already turned and was making my way out the door.

Again I made my way back to the station. As I walked into my office, Barritt was standing there, waiting for me. Much like Day had done earlier, Barritt went on the attack. 'You don't know what you're talking about. Get your facts right.'

In time I would get used to hearing those sentences from Barritt. He prefaced most of his remarks to me and other police officers, to crooks, to anyone he had a disagreement with that way. And Barritt was a disagreeable bastard.

'What I told you, I told you in confidence,' I said to Barritt. 'You've broken that confidentiality.'

He glared back at me, his massive frame looming over me. 'There was another priest whose name was John Day. He was the priest at Apollo Bay. So get your bloody facts right.'

He stormed back to his office.

I had received my first insight into the association between Barritt and Day. It was obvious to me that the two men were more than just friends. I would learn that Barritt was Day's protector, and somehow Day was able to manipulate Barritt and get whatever he wanted out of him.

As an avid member of the Catholic Mafia, Barritt understood that the Church must be protected at all costs. I would also learn that Barritt's protection extended to keeping Day's prolific child sex crimes unreported and unacknowledged.

That was the way it would be between Barritt and me from that moment on.

It turned out that Detective Sergeant James Patrick Barritt was a big fan of J. Edgar Hoover. Barritt collected clippings and ravenously read anything he could get his hands on about the FBI boss. He worshipped the man. At Mildura police station he would often break into long rambling speeches to me and others about Hoover's pursuit of communists and other enemies of the state.

Had the two men stood side by side, Barritt would have dwarfed Hoover but, like the FBI director, he had very small feet and hands, almost comically out of proportion to the rest of his gigantic frame. I have no doubt that Barritt viewed himself as a crime fighter, a little piece of J. Edgar Hoover in Mildura, with the same no-nonsense approach to bringing offenders to justice.

Like Hoover, Barritt's pursuit of criminals was entirely arbitrary. He ignored the most egregious examples of wrongdoing by his benefactor, Day, but when it came to locking up drunks, he had no peer.

I have no idea what Barritt would have made of Hoover's lifelong devotion to Freemasonry, or the gossip about Hoover's transvestism and homosexuality. Presumably, Barritt regarded these accusations as the outrages of rabble-rousers, a term he used to describe anyone who opposed his political or religious views.

Barritt even used the term to describe people who held views on chickens that were contrary to his. He was an ardent chook breeder. He had bloody big chooks, too. The scuttlebutt around Mildura was that he might have given them a touch up every now and then. If so, it certainly accounted for their large size.

I never went to Barritt's home for a meal nor as a guest. I was never invited nor would I have wanted to go, but there were occasions where I was obliged to call in on police business.

The first time I visited the Barritt home on Eighth Street, Mildura, I did so with Bill Brodie, a police reservist in the CIB office and a retired mobile traffic policeman. Bill and I knocked on the flywire door at the front of the house. After a brief wait, Barritt's wife appeared as a ghostly image through the screen. She told us that her husband was out in the backyard. It would be the only time I ever met Alma.

Bill and I walked around the back. There was this massive man, his sleeves rolled up, with an enormous chook in one hand and a hair dryer in the other, tending to the chook's coiffure. Barritt showed his chooks around the agricultural shows in the district, the Mildura Show being the main one. He took particular pride in this arcane business. The Light Sussex, a big white bird with a black speckled neck and wing tips, was his breed of choice.

At the shows Barritt raked in the prizes for his chooks. Trophies for all forms of animal husbandry were up for grabs. Breeders lucky or skilful enough to have won prizes for fat lambs, bulls or growing tomatoes or pumpkins would march off triumphantly with modest trophies in hand.

Barritt's prizes for chook breeding were far more substantial. He had seen to that, inveigling and standing over the businessmen in the district to force them to donate more glorious fare. The trophies awarded to Barritt for his chooks were the size of the Bledisloe Cup and were proudly displayed in the shop fronts in town, dwarfing the trophies in other agricultural and horticultural pursuits.

Barritt had faced the ultimate ignominy as a chook breeder—banned from showing his chooks at the Ouyen show after he had fallen for the trick of oiling his birds' feathers to give their plumage a healthy sheen. This is a distinct no-no among chook breeders, the equivalent of using performance-enhancing drugs in sports these days. The Ouyen judges called Barritt up to explain himself. The stupid bugger attended the hearing in Ouyen, arriving with a raft of legal textbooks and a compelling argument for his innocence. The judges didn't want to know and banned him on the spot. Barritt picked up his books and swept out of the room, muttering about wreaking a terrible vengeance on the judges.

But Barritt was more than a buffoon. He was a pathological liar and a fantasist.

Barritt had served with the Second AIF in New Guinea. I learnt about the stories of his heroism under fire around the Mildura traps. Barritt hadn't told me about his war service directly. He'd marked my card after I'd told him about pulling up Day back in St Kilda. Barritt viewed me as an interloper from that point on and did not take me into his confidence.

But he had told other police officers of his wartime gallantry. And the denizens of Mildura were not kept out of the loop. In the four licensed clubs in Mildura—the RSL, the Settlers, the Working Man's Club and the Mildura Club—Barritt's war stories were well known and often discussed.

Don Tripp was a detective senior constable in Mildura. He'd been in the Consorting Squad back in Melbourne. He was a tall, well built, dark-haired bloke in his mid-thirties who had been a junior state champion in amateur wrestling. He'd also been a heavyweight boxing champion in the force. I met him at Mordialloc CIB, when he came down to assist in a case I was looking after. We got on well then and continued our friendship when I transferred to Mildura. We became very solid mates.

Trippy was stationed in Mildura four years before I arrived. He disliked and mistrusted Barritt almost as much as I would come to do. I'd heard they almost came to blows behind the police station once. In the end one of the inspectors arrived and mediated the dispute. From that point on, they stayed out of each other's way.

Barritt had regaled Trippy with his war stories early in the piece. Barritt weaved tales of single-handedly overwhelming Japanese forces—a machine-gun nest overrun here, a Japanese platoon brought to heel there. It all seemed unlikely to Trippy, who was sceptical from the outset, but he was unable to refute Barritt's boasts with cold, hard evidence.

Not long after I arrived in Mildura, Trippy and I were called in to interview a man in Mildura Base Hospital. The bloke had been involved in a car accident, and uniform police had determined that the car he was driving was stolen. He'd been under police guard overnight. He was a chirpy little bloke who greeted our presence in hospital with a cheery smile.

'I know your boss,' he told us straight off the bat. 'Served with him in New Guinea.'

Trippy's eyes lit up. 'You must have seen a lot of action then.'

'Pig's arse,' the happy little car thief responded. 'We never saw a shot fired in anger.'

Trippy was getting very excited now. 'Our boss has told us different. He reckons he was in the thick of it.'

The little bloke smirked, then reached down to the cupboard beside his bed and pulled out a briefcase.

'Well, take a look at this then.' He fumbled around for a moment or two before finding a photograph and presenting it to Trippy.

'See, there's me,' he said, helpfully pointing to a face in the crowd of about a hundred Australian soldiers. Trippy and I looked at the photo: it showed an AIF company on service in New Guinea, standing ten rows abreast.

'And there's your boss,' the little bloke said, again helpfully pointing to the unmistakable image of Barritt's giant head two rows from the back. 'We never saw any Japs. Not a shot fired in anger.'

No doubt the little bloke thought he might try to get himself out of the shit he was in over the stolen car if he could just speak to his former army mate, Jim Barritt. Maybe there was a way out.

'Why don't you take me to meet your boss? I'd love to catch up with him.'

This was gold for Trippy. We weren't going to let him off, but we looked forward to being there when the little bloke caught up with his long lost brother-in-arms from New Guinea.

'We need to take you back to the station when you're medically fit to be discharged from hospital,' Trippy told him. 'The nurse tells me that will be tomorrow. So we'll come back in the morning to pick you up. You can catch up with our boss then.'

There was a gleam in Trippy's eyes and no doubt I had a glimmer in mine, too.

We went straight back to the station and walked into Barritt's office. Jim was sitting at his desk.

'How did you go?' Barritt asked.

'The bloke who knocked off that car, he reckons he's a mate of yours. Says he was in the army with you,' Trippy said, with obvious relish.

'Let me see this little pizzle,' Barritt replied.

'Pizzle' was a pejorative term Barritt used frequently. He never swore beyond 'bloody', 'bugger' and 'bastard'. Pizzle—a bull's penis—was the term he applied to anyone he disliked. And there were plenty.

The following day, Trippy and I went back to pick up our little mate. He was dressed and ready for us, beaming with good humour again. We got him back to the station and marched him straight into Barritt, who was sitting at his desk waiting for our arrival. The little bloke strode confidently up to Barritt, his hand extended in greeting.

'G'day, Jim. How are you, mate?'

Barritt ignored the offer of the little bloke's hand.

'What's this bullshit about you knowing me?' he demanded.

The little bloke reached into his briefcase and produced the photo. He leant across the desk and pointed at it with his right index finger.

'That's you, Jim. See? And that's me.'

Barritt took the photo and studied it for a moment, his brow furrowing as recognition set in. I looked across at Trippy, who was beaming with delight at Barritt's discomfort. Barritt handed the photo back and didn't say another word. Trippy and I took Barritt's old army mate back outside to the CIB office and charged him.

And that was the last we heard of Barritt's war stories.

A couple of years later I was having a beer with Stan Mornane. I'd known Stan back in Melbourne when he was a crown prosecutor. He was up in Mildura taking care of a case. He liked a beer and when in Mildura often sought out my company.

Trippy and I met up with him at the Grand Hotel on the corner of Seventh Street and Langtree Avenue, and it wasn't long before the subject turned to Barritt. Trippy told the story of the little car thief we'd charged and how he'd put Barritt's stories of wartime heroism to the flame.

'I know,' Stan said. 'I was his commanding officer in the army. He was a problem then. But I managed to work out a system to get the best out of him. I'd put him in charge of trivial stuff. I had him collecting firewood for the camp kitchens. He went about it with great enthusiasm and would start bossing people around. That was all he was good for.

I'd give him a little bit of authority and he'd be like a bull at a gate. But I'd never give him any serious job to do. That was asking too much of him.'

It was a perfect assessment of Jim Barritt.

❖

I quickly got used to the sight of George Tilley coming into the office at the end of each day. Tilley was the editor of the local newspaper, the *Sunraysia Daily*. He'd been a journalist at the *Truth* in Melbourne. I got on quite well with him. He was a solid Labor man and pretty good company. But his background at the *Truth* told me he was not a bloke I could trust. Our dealings never got beyond the social, an occasional chat over a beer. But he and Barritt would sit together in Barritt's office for hours on end, talking in low voices.

I didn't pay much attention as, more often than not, I was walking out the door at the end of my shift. But a quick glance at any copy of the *Sunraysia Daily* around that time would almost invariably contain a photo of Barritt's boofhead under a screeching headline detailing some crime that Barritt would claim to have thwarted.

It was obvious that Tilley and Barritt used each other—Tilley to get information about police activities for his newspaper and Barritt to advance his credentials as a champion of the common good. A smart bloke like Tilley nourished Barritt's gargantuan ego to get information. He saw his visits to Barritt's office as a way of keeping in touch with the gossip, innuendo and scuttlebutt of Mildura and the district.

Barritt may have been a cartoon fool but he was smart enough to realise that if he had an 'in' with the media in and around Mildura, this would add considerably to his power.

On my second day at the Mildura CIB, Trippy told me that Barritt had a show on the local radio station, 3MA. I listened in the first chance I got, eager to hear what stories of bravado Barritt would impart to a grateful township. True to form, Barritt gave his radio show the old J. Edgar Hoover treatment.

The show started with a drum roll that reached a crescendo, followed by a solemn, grave voice-over: 'And now we cross to the office of Senior Detective Jim Barritt at the Criminal Investigation Branch at Mildura.'

It was all very film noir—for Mildura local radio, that is.

'Good evening listeners,' Barritt's gruff voice would intone, 'from the thin blue line at Mildura CIB.'

I couldn't quite believe what I was hearing. This was a trumpet-blowing exercise of the most obvious kind. If it wasn't so serious I would have fallen about laughing at Barritt's antics. He used his thirty-minute spot as a strident piece of self-promotion. He told stories of crooks he'd locked up, criminal conspiracies he had foiled and his overall outstanding service to the community.

It soon became obvious that ninety per cent of it was bullshit. The arrests he referred to were made either by the uniform boys or Trippy in CIB. The conspiracies were contrived and his service to the community was invariably self-serving.

Sometimes he would use his radio show to even up old scores. I remember he had a particular grudge against a publican in Ouyen who bore the unfortunate surname of Greed.

'There is a Gree-eedy man south of Mildura who is causing great consternation regarding the licensing laws of Victoria. I want this man to know that I will catch up with him sooner rather than later and, when I do, he will come off second best. To this man I say, "I am watching you."'

God only knows what the man had done. I met him years later and he seemed like a decent bloke and a good publican. But he had banged heads with Jim Barritt, who could not let that go unpunished.

Before I arrived in Mildura, Barritt used his radio show to announce that I was on my way up from Melbourne. Over the course of three or four weeks, Mildura's airwaves resounded to his description of me as an outstanding investigator, a good family man and a devout Catholic who would be an asset to the community. In his gruff voice, he painted me as an Eliot Ness on my way to assist Barritt in his never-ending crusade against crime.

If I had known I would have cringed with embarrassment. I only found out when Trippy gave me a heads up.

'Before you came up, Barritt was blowing his bags about what a fine man, great detective and policeman you are,' Trippy told me. 'The uniformed boys and I were suspicious of you. We thought you were going to be a carbon copy of him.'

❖

The Victoria Police force has always been an Australian Labor Party (ALP) stronghold. It goes back to the days of Ned Kelly, maybe before. Police were paid atrocious wages and the Police Association—the police trade union—struggled hard to achieve better wages and conditions. The unions and the ALP work hand in glove. The Police Association supported the ALP for the most part, and most members of the force followed suit.

I'd been a Labor voter all my life. I was brought up in a strict Labor family. My father was an active unionist during the Depression and copped more than his fair share of beatings from union busters and thugs.

In 1955 the Australian Labor Party split along sectarian and ideological lines. In New South Wales, the Catholic Church opposed the split, but in Victoria the schism was driven by the meddling of St Patrick's Cathedral and Archbishop Daniel Mannix with his puppet, Bob Santamaria. The Catholic Right in Victoria was made up of white-collar unionists and professional types. Its political wing after the split was the Democratic Labor Party (DLP). Santamaria was the head of the National Civic Council, the administrative and fund-raising wing of the DLP. Like the rest of the Catholic Right in the state, he was virulently anti-communist.

I was no fan of communism either but, unlike Santamaria, I did not see Soviet-style communism as a threat to our way of life in Australia. Santamaria was a zealot with far too much influence on Australian politics. I was also disgusted with Mannix's influence on the ALP, and once the split occurred I thought the members of the DLP had set the labour movement on a path to oblivion. I had no doubt that the DLP took its orders either directly or indirectly from Mannix and his henchmen. It was during these years of despair that I voted Liberal twice, but my allegiances eventually returned to the ALP.

It was in those heady days that I had my only real political discussion with Jim Barritt. As usual, it didn't take long for Barritt to express his views and dismiss mine. The trigger for his outburst was a discussion in the CIB office on capital punishment. Don Tripp, like me, was a Labor man and, like me, was stridently opposed to hanging. He liked to needle Barritt and knew the topic would quickly draw a response from him.

'When are Victorian politicians going to get around to repealing the death penalty? This is 1962,' Trippy said, casting an eye in Barritt's direction.

'It's barbarity,' I responded.

'You blokes don't know what you're talking about,' Barritt said with his usual tact. 'Hang the bastards. That's what they deserve.'

'What about the innocent fellas?' I asked. 'You want to hang them as well?'

'There's no capital punishment across the river,' Trippy chimed in.

'It's Labor policy,' I said. 'A change of government in Victoria and that'd be the end of it.'

'You blokes don't know what you're talking about. Labor Party! Bunch of bloody commos. We're just bloody lucky that we've got a man like Bob Santamaria keeping the red bastards at bay.'

Barritt was a fanatical Catholic. I believed in the faith of the Church but Barritt's belief stretched only to its politics. He attended church for mass almost every day, but Sunday would be enough for me, and I'd see him there then.

In any mass, donations are sought at two points in the service. The plate is first passed around for donations for the welfare of the priest. Later in the service, the plate is passed around again. This dough, designated for the church's building funds and for consolidated funds in the diocese, would more often than not come in envelopes.

Barritt was one of four parishioners charged with the responsibility of collecting donations. The big man would strut down the centre aisle with a pious look on his face, peering down as each parishioner reached into their pockets and placed their contributions on the plate. Not a word was ever spoken but Barritt's eyebrows would rise slightly if he deemed that a parishioner was not forthcoming or not sufficiently generous. These weren't donations. The parishioners were being stood over, extorted by this big copper.

Barritt was a fool. It did not take me long to figure out that he was also a dangerous one.

In Barritt's opinion there were 'Catholics and other bastards'. In church he might stand over Catholics with the collection plate in hand, but he regarded everyone else in Mildura with deep suspicion.

Driven by his strident Catholicism and the exhortations of Mannix and Santamaria, Barritt had become an agent for the Australian Security Intelligence Organisation (ASIO). This was a very murky business to say the least.

Mildura was a seething mass of ethnic and cultural backgrounds. Its population at the time was a melting pot of Italians, Greeks and people from the Balkan states—all fleeing the privations of post-war Europe—mingled with the white Anglo-Saxon faces, most of whom had come to Mildura after World War I on government farmer settlement programs for war veterans.

Everyone who was settled in Mildura at the time had come to start a new life. Many had come to the town to avoid persecution or hardship. Some had come to escape an uncertain future in other parts of the world. Some, too, had come to avoid the harsh light of scrutiny—fugitives from the big cities of Sydney, Adelaide and Melbourne.

Barritt himself was a refugee of a kind, having been dispatched from Melbourne, where he had become an embarrassment to the Victoria Police force. His heavy-handedness as a uniformed sergeant in Footscray had led to complaints. There was a story floating around Mildura that he had belted the wrong man, the son of a Victorian parliamentarian. The son's story of a physical assault and violence at the hands of Barritt got back to the MP, who had the pull to get senior police to look into Barritt's activities.

In any event, Barritt was sent north to Mildura, effectively in exile. For the force, it was a case of out of sight, out of mind. Provided there were no outrages, no cries of scandal or disgrace heard in Melbourne, Barritt was free to establish his own personal fiefdom in Mildura.

With his ASIO hat on, Barritt would bully and intimidate ethnic groups in the district and beyond, wherever his CIB duties would take him. He developed a network of informers in the Italian, Balkan and Greek communities in Mildura, and would inveigle information of the most trivial kind from them, then embellish these morsels into vast conspiracies in his reports to the intelligence agency.

God only knows what ASIO made of these reports. I dare say most of Barritt's intelligence would have found its way into the bin in Canberra, but it didn't stop him banging out reports to ASIO. Sometimes I'd see him in his office in the wee hours of the morning, hammering away on his old typewriter like his very existence depended on it.

He was obsessed with the Mafia and believed that the international criminal cartel had reached deeply into Mildura. It was a nonsense, another part of his contrived J. Edgar Hoover persona.

Hoover had ignored the existence of the Mafia in the United States until 1957, when a copper chanced across a lot of sleek black limousines inexplicably parked outside a farmhouse in the sleepy village of Apalachin, New York. Hoover had been stung into acceptance, if not action, from that point on.

Barritt, the cartoon crime fighter who doted on Hoover, didn't need his own Apalachin moment. He thought if you shook a tree around Mildura, a Mafia capo with a violin case in his hand would fall out.

Imagined crimes, where he saw himself as the heroic upholder of the right, were Barritt's go. It was the real ones, the sexual assaults against children, he chose to ignore, perverting the course of justice to shield the paedophile John Day.

❖

Sergeant Michael O'Donnell was one of the uniform boys who'd come up from Melbourne with his young family, looking for a new life. Mick was a big lump of a bloke, a former champion surf lifesaver in Melbourne and the first of the force's frogmen in the Search and Rescue Squad.

Mick was a self-effacing copper who'd lived a life of adventure in the navy and then the police. He'd been a CIB detective in Melbourne. I'd worked with him out of Russell Street. His sister, Kath, had married my old senior officer, the straight-laced, tough Detective Sergeant Jack Meehan.

Mick had got back into uniform, was promoted to sergeant and transferred to Mildura. His wife had family in the district, including an uncle in Ouyen. Like me, he had come to Mildura unaware of the dark force of nature that was Jim Barritt.

Mick's surname preceded him to Mildura and Barritt, the Catholic bigot, must have rubbed his hands together, thinking he had another like mind on his way up to bolster the town's Catholic Mafia.

Barritt would discover that assumption is the mother of all stuff-ups. Despite the Irish name, Mick O'Donnell was a lapsed Catholic who had married a Protestant and become a Freemason. His wife's uncle in Ouyen was the grandmaster of the local lodge. Barritt knew none of this at the time. When Mick arrived, Barritt, expecting another member of the 'one of us club', took Mick to his heart and showed him around the traps, introducing him to Joe Kearney, clerk of the courts, and Joe Hayes, the magistrate who was in Mildura at the time. The excursion with Barritt took longer than expected and Mick did not get the grand introduction to Father John Day, as I did.

Somewhere along the line, one of Barritt's confreres let it be known that he had met Mick at the annual Freemason's picnic at Ouyen and that Mick's wife's uncle was a bigwig in the local Masons. And that was the end of the conviviality between Mick and Barritt. From 'one of us', Mick became 'one of them', and Barritt went out of his way to make Mick's time in Mildura as difficult as he could.

One minor infringement of the police regulations—an 'i' not dotted or a 't' not crossed—and Barritt would fire off a report to the inspector. But Mick was a very good police officer. I didn't give a damn about his associations outside the force.

Mick had received a complaint from a Mildura local. The man's young son was in grade six at Sacred Heart Primary School. The boy had come home from school one day to tell his dad that Father John Day had set upon him, pinned him down and fondled his penis.

It was a serious complaint—a CIB matter—and Mick referred it to Trippy. Trippy told Mick that it was not the first time he had received complaints about Day for sexually assaulting young children, mainly boys. Almost apologetically, Trippy informed Mick that these complaints were invariably snaffled by Barritt. Trippy wasn't allowed to touch them. It was all part of the agreement that Trippy had with Barritt, so they would stay out of each other's way. Any complaint against Day went straight to Barritt.

In the normal course of events, a uniform police officer would simply approach the detective and follow up on the complaint—ask the detective what had transpired. But Barritt was such an unapproachable bastard that the uniform boys rarely did this. And Barritt had been bullying and picking on Mick ever since he had arrived in Mildura.

Having heard nothing, and not wanting to have another scrap with the obdurate Barritt, Mick went straight out to the complainant's home to ask what was going on. The bloke told him straight out that Barritt had come around to his house and talked him into withdrawing the complaint. Barritt had painted a picture of untold scandal and shame, and told him that his boy had made serious allegations against a good man and a fine priest. The Catholic Church would not take that lying down. Sound and fury and the wrath of God were to be expected if the man proceeded with the complaint. The man felt he had no choice but to withdraw the complaint. Mick asked him if he was willing to reinstate it, but the man steadfastly refused.

There was nothing Mick could do but now he had an inkling of Day's secret crimes against children. Trippy had told him that this was not the first time Barritt had stood over an anxious parent who had learnt that his son or daughter had been abused by Day.

Neither Mick nor Trippy ever told me about these complaints or about how Barritt had intervened and let Day off the hook. But in 2006, Mick published his memoirs, *A Little Bit O' Luck*, a collection of mostly amusing anecdotes of his life. He sent me a copy with a note inside the front cover written in his own hand.

'Here you go, Dinny. There are parts in this book that will interest you,' the note from Mick read.

I was thunderstruck when I read it. It was evidence of Day's paedophilia and confirmation of Barritt's collusion with Day, protecting this vile priest from the reach of the law, and a succinct rebuttal of Barritt's subsequent denials of any knowledge of Day's disgusting abuse of children.

Why had Mick and Trippy not acted? Why had they not taken these complaints further, over Barritt's head and up the chain of command? And why didn't they tell me? Perhaps they saw me as one of the Catholic Mafia, or maybe they thought that because of my faith I would be disinclined to pursue Day. They were wrong about that. But they knew the Victoria Police better than I did. Mick and Trippy concluded that the slithering, crawling contents of that particular can would be better left unopened.

When my turn came, I determined that the can would be opened and the worms, grubs and maggots therein held up to the light. And in doing so, I lost it all—my career, my pension, my wife, my health and my sanity.

❖

Barritt was a member of the Catholic Mafia in Mildura, though the organisational structure may not have been as complex as the Mafia in the United States. Barritt's mafia was designed on an equilateral triangular structure, with Day—the spiritual leader of the dark, perverse group—at the top; Barritt on the right-hand vertex below; and opposite Barritt, Joe Kearney. Kearney was the law; Barritt, the order.

Barritt and Kearney were foot soldiers for Day. Barritt was Day's minder while the opportunist Kearney was his money man. Together they offered Day protection and, within the confines of the Mildura district, almost unfettered power. Barritt had the police stitched up, and Kearney, the courts. Day was free to do as he pleased. It was a dirty, corrupt triumvirate, an unholy trinity with Day at the forefront.

Joe Kearney was the clerk of the courts, a position of no great consequence in Melbourne, but in a country town like Mildura at that time he had greater status and authority. Without a sitting magistrate in the district, Kearney was the most senior officer of the court in Mildura.

Joe Hayes was the circuit magistrate who appeared in Mildura when necessary, but he would preside over matters in the town and then move on to other courts in his district—Ararat, Stawell, Horsham. Then Kearney was left to his own devices. In a country town like Mildura, a man like Kearney could impose himself as a person of almost untold authority—judge and jury all in one.

Kearney was a short, solidly built man with thick, wavy brown hair, parted on the left-hand side. There wasn't a time where I didn't see him without a cigarette dangling from his lips. He was a chain smoker and heavy whisky drinker who would help himself to his first glass of the day before the sun was over the yardarm.

Despite the ash that would fleck and speckle his suit pants throughout the day, every morning Kearney could be seen at his desk, neatly dressed, the ash gone as if its presence the previous day had been an apparition, the pleat on his trousers razor sharp. His appearance would degenerate throughout the day, as if his clothes had begun to reflect the stains of his own personal moral decay.

He'd been a good Australian Rules footballer, or so I had been told. He walked with a marked limp, and the story was that he'd done his left knee while chasing a football around the park when he was a young man.

Kearney had a staff of three—two male assistants and a female—and he ruled the court with the air of a tyrant. He was a deviant and a fraud. With a lofty air, he dispensed free legal advice to anyone who sought it and to many who didn't.

Kearney oversaw all matters relating to the function of the Mildura Court. This included the dispensation of court-ordered family maintenance payments to women in Mildura who were divorced.

It was not easy being a single mother in those days. And the plight of these women was made a good deal more difficult by Kearney. He would make them endure his abhorrent jokes and lewd remarks before he would deign to hand over their cheques. The cheques belonged to the women anyway, but he had them bluffed into believing that he held absolute discretion over how much they would be paid or indeed if they would be paid at all. The women were fearful and intimidated, and would not report him. They believed that Kearney held the key to their financial wellbeing.

If I had known that he was monstering women, I would have been all over him—locked him up, charged him and put him through the courts he purported to represent, but everything was hushed up by his office.

God only knows the dread these poor women suffered at the thought of having to visit Kearney to get the measly amounts of money that was their due anyway. At some point, Kearney's behaviour towards women took a turn for the worse: he raped a woman in his office. She fled, having fought Kearney off, but would not report the incident to the police. He had control of her maintenance payments and, in her mind, Kearney held the power of her very existence in his hands. She could not challenge him.

Kearney held the keys to the court's coffers. It wasn't just maintenance payments. There were also costs awarded in the course of prosecutions and fines imposed by the court to be paid out. Kearney had access to them all. He had deluded himself into believing that the money was his. That delusion is a small step away from fraud, and it appears Kearney made the move effortlessly. By my estimate, he had been rorting court funds for two decades.

Kearney was a Catholic, too, but he was not an overtly pious man like Barritt. He seemed to view the Catholic Church as a kind of social club, a club he wanted to be in the midst of in order to impose himself and reap some personal rewards. That was how Joe Kearney found himself as treasurer of Mildura Catholic Church parish funds and Father John Day's bagman.

Kearney was also treasurer of the parish council, overseeing all funds for the parish. This included funds paid by the Commonwealth government for the administration and maintenance of the Catholic primary and secondary schools in the parish. These were substantial amounts of money set aside for teaching resources, curriculum development, building maintenance and teachers' salaries.

Kearney knew a rort when he saw one. Like most rorts, it was all terribly easy. He simply created a non-existent teacher's position at Sacred Heart School, the Catholic primary school adjacent to the Mildura church. Then he hired a teacher who did not exist. When the Commonwealth government dutifully paid the salary to this 'teacher', Kearney was there, sticking the money in his kick.

Some of the money no doubt ended up in Kearney's back pocket, but the bulk of it was given to Father John Day to keep him in his American cars, fine wines and imported Scotch, and to pay for his prostitutes.

Day was one of the Catholic Church's builders. That was why he was held in such regard. Every parish he called home—and there were many—would see him badgering parishioners for money to build churches and extend existing ones into vast monoliths. Not for the glorification of God: it was all for the glorification of Father John Day and the Catholic Church. Day considered it his duty to extort funds from anyone prepared to pay up, and he and Kearney oversaw the collection of money and dispersed it as they saw fit.

It wasn't the only rort they had going. The church building fund was another shakedown that Kearney and Day used as their own personal slush fund.

The notion of sacrificial giving wasn't new to Mildura's Catholic parishioners, but Kearney and Day took it to the level of extortion. Every Sunday, Day would bully and berate parishioners to empty their pockets, not just into the collection plates that Barritt would stomp down the aisle with, but also in letters demanding donations for the building fund. They didn't get a cracker from me but many Catholics in Mildura were swayed by Day's constant exhortations for more and more money.

Every couple of months Day arranged trips down to Melbourne for some of the wealthier parishioners in Mildura. They would stay at Melbourne's original four-star hotel, the Southern Cross Hotel, on the Saturday night and return to Mildura the following day. It was all part of the fund-raising drive and Day was up front that the church building fund would receive a cut from the hotel on the bookings.

On one occasion, one of Mildura's prominent businessmen was startled to be approached by Day as he was checking into the hotel.

'Let's have some fun tonight,' Day said. 'I know a brothel where we can really go to town.'

'No, thanks,' the businessman said, startled and clearly aghast at the idea of hitting a brothel with a priest. 'I'm not really interested, Father.' The man's wife was less than a few steps away.

Day routinely treated women with contempt. He threatened and cajoled the various women's groups attached to the parish to work harder and harder on their fund raising and hand over more and more money to Kearney.

Day used to dote on an Airedale terrier. Sometimes women visited Day on the front verandah of the presbytery on some church errand or other. He would come out and talk to them while his dog would sniff away at their genitals before becoming excited and clambering up to start humping their legs.

Day regarded this as the height of comedy. Instead of rebuking the dog and ordering it to stop, he would stand back and grin, delighting in the women's discomfort. Some women played his game, eager to ingratiate themselves to God's soldier on earth in their local parish, but most of the women despised and distrusted him.

When I arrived in this moral cesspit, Day was raping and assaulting children, in Mildura and elsewhere. He had been doing it before I arrived and he would do it for more than a decade afterwards, until his first victim came forward.

It was his lust for money and his bullying of parishioners that first cast light on his paedophilia. The parishioners eventually tired of Day's grasping ways and, one by one, his crimes were forced out of the shadows.

❖

My wife Jean converted to Catholicism in 1964. I'd never placed any pressure on her to do this; her religion was her business. It was something of a surprise that she did so.

One evening after I got home from work, she pulled me aside and told me she'd had a number of meetings with Father Laurie Halloran, a priest at the presbytery under John Day. Seven months pregnant with our fourth child, Anthony, she had taken instruction from O'Halloran, the first step in becoming a Catholic.

I had no idea that she had been doing this but I was very pleased. It was a considerable effort on her part—a way of making the most of her new life in Mildura. I took it as a sign that our marriage was stronger than ever.

Shortly afterwards, Jean was confirmed and began attending mass with the boys and me at Mildura Catholic Church. We went to mass as a family every Sunday from that point on. The church would fill before the 10 am service with 200 or so members of the congregation vying for the best seats. We would get there early with the kids and take up our regular spots in a pew alongside the confessionals.

At any time there were as many as four or five priests at Mildura under Day. A roster system was in place for the priests and any one of them might conduct the Sunday morning mass. I wasn't especially bothered when I'd see Day at the pulpit. I didn't like him but I didn't have to. I'd grown up respecting priests, but I didn't have to enjoy their company. My faith was a private matter and mass was an exercise of that. I regarded the priests, including Day, as a means of achieving my own spiritual ends.

I knew enough about Day not to swallow the line that priests were Christ's representatives on earth. A lot of other Catholics might have thought differently, but for me a priest was only a conduit for my faith. My faith was a complete democracy and not ruled by the Vatican's edicts.

One Sunday, his pious fuming concluded for another week, Day invited the congregation to kneel and pray in private meditation.

I sat with Jean to my left, while the children sat next to her. Michael first, followed by Martin and Gavin in age order.

'Look after Jean and the boys,' I murmured to myself. 'Make sure they're all right.'

I looked up at the altar with its depiction of the crucifixion—a plaster Christ on the wooden cross. The hands and feet of Christ were brushed with red paint to signify the stigmata and the wound on the right side of the chest. I saw blood suddenly gush from the wound on the chest, flowing on to the legs and dripping on the floor in a puddle half a metre wide. I stared at the altar for several moments. It didn't frighten me. I felt no sense of apprehension either. I just kept looking. Finally I turned to Jean.

'Did you see that?'

'What?' she replied, stirring from her own meditation.

'On the cross. The blood.'

Jean looked back at me, blinking. 'No.'

I looked back at the altar and the blood was gone. The puddle had vanished and the blood that streamed down had stopped. No doubt some will say the vision must have some rational explanation. I don't know. I only know what I saw.

What did it mean? I don't know that either. I didn't feel compelled to bear arms in a holy war or to run off and join a monastery. I didn't feel charged with a supernatural power to go and fight injustice wherever it occurred. I only know what I saw.

What I didn't appreciate then was that if ever there was a place where Christ was wanted, it was Mildura in 1964. The psychologists might call Day a psychopath and point to his grandiosity, his self-importance, his capacity for manipulation and his heightened arousal in seeing children in pain and trauma. I prefer to think of him as a bastard of the lowest order. How else could I explain a man who would attempt to sodomise a boy in the presbytery, ejaculating all over the boy's buttocks and thighs on a Friday afternoon, then turn up on Sunday to conduct mass and offer some thumping sermon on the lowering of moral standards, the sin of abortion and the decadence of girls who had taken to wearing miniskirts?

Father Day could pull off this gross feat of hypocrisy with ease, in such a way that the congregation, including myself, would remain blissfully ignorant for many years. He'd been doing it since he'd arrived in Mildura in 1956. He'd been doing it all over western Victoria under the nose of the Ballarat diocese for decades longer.

Children were bowed into silence and dread; parents were rendered servile by the power that Day, and his henchmen, Barritt and Kearney, wielded in their community.

I knew Day was a dedicated pervert. The vision of him in St Kilda stayed with me, returning every time he harangued the congregation from the pulpit, either demanding money or wagging a cautionary finger about the decline of morality. I'd switch off during his sermonic rants, turning my mind to the preceding day's cricket and the runs I did or didn't make. I couldn't be bothered listening to him.

4

CONFESSIONS

See everything, overlook a great deal, correct a little.
POPE JOHN XXIII, 1881–1963

Often three or four priests lived at the presbytery at Mildura under Day. They would come and go, filling in at parishes within the district when called upon. There was Father Laurie Halloran, Father Leslie Sheahan, Father Daniel Arundell. And there was a tall, solidly built, gregarious priest by the name of Father Gerald Ridsdale. He was based at Mildura from June 1964 to October 1966.

I don't remember much about him. He was known to turn up at parishioners' homes with a chop in a plastic bag around meal times. He'd be welcomed into their homes and his chop cooked up with all the trimmings.

Ridsdale is regarded as one of the most prolific paedophiles the world has ever seen. He has admitted to raping children on 'hundreds' of occasions. He has been convicted of seventy-five separate counts of indecent assault, nine counts of buggery and numerous counts of gross indecency.

He is in the eighteenth year of a prison sentence and is due for parole in 2013, when he will be 79 years of age.

During his first court appearance in 1993, Ridsdale entered court with Cardinal—then Bishop—George Pell at his side. Ridsdale and Pell had known each other when they were priests in the Ballarat diocese. Ridsdale's victims in court were left to wonder why Pell was there to offer his old priestly mate some moral support but had nothing to say to *them*.

There is no doubt in my mind that Day, like Ridsdale, subjected hundreds of children to rape and sexual assaults. But, unlike Ridsdale, Day would never have his moment of reckoning. Not on this earth at any rate. Both were protected by the bishops of Ballarat—first James O'Collins, then Ronald Mulkearns. When the stories of Day's and Ridsdale's crimes against children grew too loud to ignore, these bishops transferred the priests to other parishes and other communities.

These two predatory priests left thousands of shattered lives across western Victoria. Yet Day progressed through the Church because he was seen as one of its builders. Ridsdale was an embarrassment, a nobody. Day, however, was valued.

Unlike Ridsdale, who never rose higher than a simple priest in the Catholic Church, Day was feted by the Roman Catholic Church and promoted through the ranks—a priest, then a parish priest in Ararat, Horsham, Beech Forest and Apollo Bay. Each time, when the whispers grew too loud for Bishop O'Collins's liking, Ridsdale had been sent packing. But Day was not exiled. Instead he was promoted first to dean and then, in 1967, to monsignor, essentially second in charge to the bishop himself. The next step for Day was a bishop's mitre.

❖

I'd been taking the sacrament of penance or confession since I was 10 years old. It is part of the ritual of being a Roman Catholic. Once a month I would sit in the darkened confessional and wait for the priest to pull the shutter and hear me give an account of my mortal sins over the previous month.

'Forgive me, Father, for I have sinned . . .'

Mortal sins are shaped by the Ten Commandments—a breach of any of the ten would see a Roman Catholic peering through a screen, seeking absolution from a more or less anonymous priest. The serious crimes of murder and theft are included in the Ten Commandments. I had nothing to confess in that respect. There were other sins of no great moment. I might have played cricket instead of going to mass or used the odd profanity in the course of my work, and these would find me genuflecting, requesting forgiveness every month or so.

Confession was a pain for me. It was something I had to do. It was just another one of the man-made laws associated with my religion, part of the habit of Catholicism.

While I was a detective in Melbourne, I spent a whole day trying to make a confession and still came up short. I was due to give evidence at the County Court in the morning and made my way to St Francis Church in Lonsdale Street on the way to court from Russell Street. The queue of sinners was a mile long. I couldn't hang around so I headed off to court.

During the lunch recess I walked back to St Francis, and again there was a long wait for confession. There must have been a profusion of sin in Melbourne at the time. I headed back to court.

It was after four o'clock when the court went into recess for the day. Again I made my way to St Francis. I expected to find another long line of sinners seeking penance but this time I was in luck. I walked in just as a redeemed sinner was making his way out of the confessional.

I quickly took his place and got down on my knees.

'Forgive me, Father, for I have sinned.'

There was silence.

'Forgive me Father, for I have sinned,' I repeated.

This time there was a response, but not one I expected. I heard a yawn from the other side of the screen and then the tell-tale whistle of an elderly man in deep slumber. The priest had fallen asleep. After that, I decided I wasn't going to catalogue my sins during confession. If I had sins, why should I seek absolution from another human being, albeit a priest? If I wanted forgiveness I could shout it out to the heavens. God was always listening, or so we were told.

At my next confession, I walked into the confessional at St Francis's. The screen opened.

'Forgive me, Father, for I have sinned,' I said.

The priest leaned forward.

'Go on, my son.'

'That's it. I've sinned,' I replied.

'Oh. All right,' the priest stammered. 'Say three Our Fathers and ten Hail Marys. Off you go. Next.'

And that was it. Done and dusted. Sins purged. Off I went.

When I did go to confession at the Mildura church, I would scan the board inside to determine which priest was hearing confessions. I may well have offered my confession to Gerard Ridsdale at some point. I don't remember it, but it's possible. The idea of it appals me. At the time I wouldn't have been worried about Ridsdale. My main purpose was to dodge Day. So I'd look at the list and if Day was on it, I'd be straight out the door.

But one day, I didn't check and marched straight into the confessional.

'Forgive me, Father, for I have sinned,' I said to the amorphous image beyond the screen.

'Yes, my son,' came the response in Day's unmistakable voice, replete with just a hint of his characteristic affected English accent.

'Forgive me, Father, for I have sinned,' I repeated, kicking myself that I was stuck there in front of Day.

'Is that all?' he enquired.

'Yes. I have sinned.'

'Do you want to give me some details?' Day asked.

'No.'

'All right. Say three Our Fathers and ten Hail Marys.'

And that was the last time I ever went to confession. I knew I was a better man than Day. Why should I be seeking forgiveness from him? Why should I have to endure penance dispensed by this man?

Confession had become a production line of moral ablution. It was a means of subjugating Catholics—an intimate invasion of their privacy—and it gave priests knowledge and thus power over their parishioners. A priest taking confession is obliged to regard the admissions of those who offer them in the strictest confidence. This creates one of the numerous clashes between the law of the land and Church law, and poses a veritable mountain of moral quandaries.

If a priest hears a confession from a person who plans to commit a murder in the future, is the priest bound by the law to notify the police? If a priest takes confession from a man who has committed a serious crime and the priest declines to notify the authorities, is that priest guilty of conspiracy or being an accessory after the fact?

The answer, in short, is grey and uncertain, and depends on the degree of desire of secular law in a particular jurisdiction to override canon law. That most jurisdictions show little or no desire to challenge canon law reveals the distinct power of the Catholic Church in the Christian world.

To this day, in Victoria, a priest cannot be compelled to give evidence in a trial based on admissions made in the confessional.

But the confessional door swings both ways. Those Catholics who meekly offer their sins in return for absolution leave their dark and sometimes dirty secrets in the bosom of the clergy. It is an intrinsic form of control, and in the hands of a priest like Father John Day, it becomes a tacit form of blackmail and extortion, and can lead to a punishment of a more earthly nature.

Day would listen to the confessions of all parishioners at one time or another—men, women and children. He held their secrets close but not so close that he would not share them with his enforcer and right-hand man, Jim Barritt.

CONFESSIONS

The nuns who taught at Sacred Heart Primary School would take the children out of class and march them across the playground and into the church. Grade six one day, grade five another, all the way down to the 5-year-olds in prep class.

The kids would sit outside the confessionals and walk up one by one with the woebegone air of condemned men. They had all been told that a life without confession and absolution would mean eternal damnation, fire, brimstone and an abominable hell in the afterlife. Many of the children would quiver in fear, eager to purge themselves of their guilt. Most had nothing to feel guilty about. There were some who had fallen off the path of righteousness in the way that children do from time to time. Some had stolen an orange from an orchard. Some had swiped lollies at the local milk bar. Some had broken into the pavilion at the local sports ground and helped themselves to the soft drinks.

Day would listen to their trembling confessions and demand penance in a severe voice. These kids, minor offenders at worst, left the confessional thinking the slate had been wiped clean.

But Day would breach their confidence and take their confessions directly to Detective Sergeant Jim Barritt. The next thing the kids knew, Barritt was around at their homes, banging on their doors and taking them back to the police station to interview them in the company of their parents.

Any decent police officer would have had a stern word to the kids in their homes, in front of their parents. That would generally be enough to pull them back on the right track. Not Jim Barritt. He'd charge these kids—10, 12 years of age—and bring them before the Children's Court. More often than not the court would issue the kids with a warning. Generally no convictions were recorded. Nevertheless, the grim process of being charged and appearing in court under summons were stains that lasted a lifetime.

In this way, Barritt got his arrest rates up, despite the fact that these were pinches of a pathetically trivial nature. He also managed to impose himself on the community as a person to be feared, especially by young people.

Barritt was in and out of the Mildura Catholic Church virtually every day. He had his moments in the confessional with Day, too. Barritt had plenty to confess. His lies, his corruption, his bullying and the contents of the top drawer of his office desk. In the confessional, Day would hang on every word.

The bagman, Joe Kearney, had much to confess, too—his rape of women, his fraud—and Day would carefully note Kearney's sins and consign them to his memory for possible future reference.

In this way, Day was able to control and wield power over Barritt and Kearney.

But who took Monsignor John Day's confession?

❖

Barritt's office took up the largest room in the CIB. Trippy's desk and mine were in another room, separated by the fingerprint room. Barritt's office was unspectacular. He had his desk, a bookcase behind his chair and a couple of filing cabinets in the corner near the door. In the opposite corner, next to his desk, sat the CIB safe under lock and key.

Safes are common in police stations, especially out in the country. Firearms—usually three pistols and a box of bullets—were stored there. Occasionally very valuable evidentiary items—large sums of cash or expensive jewellery—would also be stored there, but for the most part evidence would be deposited in the property room.

Barritt's safe was always locked tight. He had the only key and kept it in his kick at all times. If we ever needed to get our firearms, we had to find him in one of his haunts and then get the third degree on whether we needed them or not. The top right-hand drawer of Barritt's desk also remained locked, but all CIB detectives needed to have access to the safe.

Trippy and I developed a fascination about the contents of the safe and the top drawer. We speculated that Barritt kept his ASIO files in the safe, but what else? If we could just take a look, we figured we'd find an Aladdin's Cave of clandestine treasures, an insight into his secrets and perhaps a mirror on his dark soul.

We never got into the safe. I still wonder about what might have been in there. But the top drawer would prove easier to open.

'We have to get into that top drawer,' I told Trippy in the office one day.

'I'd love to know,' he replied. Then a gleam came into his eye.

'You know I'm going to Melbourne next week? All I need is the code and I can get a key cut at the government supply.'

'I think that's a very good idea, Trippy,' I said.

Barritt was out of the office so we had our chance. We both crept into Barritt's office, mindful that he could return at any time. Trippy pulled on the drawer but it remained locked, as we expected. He crouched down and got a look at the number of the lock, then jotted it down on a notepad.

When he got back from his trip to the big smoke, Trippy fronted me in the office. He pulled a key out of his pocket and dangled it in front of my face, grinning like a madman.

We waited for Barritt to leave the office, then checked that the coast was clear. I closed the door to the CIB. Trippy and I were a bit toey. You never knew when Barritt would be in and out of the office. He never let anyone know where he was going or when he'd be back.

Trippy put the key in the lock of the drawer and turned it. We were in.

Inside the top drawer were a few loose papers. I glanced at them quickly and realised they were of no great significance. But underneath the papers were five black and white photographs of prepubescent girls between 8 and 10 years old. They were all completely naked and standing front to the camera, with glum, expressionless faces and their genitals showing.

If these had been evidence, they would have been entered in the property book and stored in the property office.

'These are perv's photos,' Trippy said, casting his eyes over them.

It was true. They had not been professionally taken. Amateur stuff, but it was still child pornography.

We quickly put the photos back, then closed and locked the drawer.

Why Barritt kept child pornography under lock and key was a mystery, and would remain so. We knew Barritt was an unusual man, but now we knew he was also a pervert. The evidence was building.

❖

Joe Hayes, the circuit magistrate, had been calling in to Mildura to hear cases. The life of a circuit magistrate could be lonely—sitting in hotel rooms, eating alone. If he went for a beer, he'd he looking over his shoulder for blokes he might have had before him.

I'd gotten to know Joe pretty well through matters I prosecuted in court. We at least had one thing in common. He did not like Kearney. I can't recall him saying anything positive about Barritt.

Joe was a very proper magistrate. I never heard him swear. He was a short, serious little man suffering from the early onset of male pattern baldness. He spoke slowly and softly, as if weighing the import of every word before he uttered it. He may well have been prone to shyness as a young man but his role as magistrate did not allow him to shrink from view. In his slightly awkward, detached manner, he carried an air of authority.

I felt a bit sorry for Joe, tucked away in his room on his own, so I'd invite him over to our place. Jean would cook a roast and we'd all tuck in over a bottle of red. After the kids had gone to bed, Jean would sit in the lounge room and watch TV, and Joe and I would chat about this and that—football, politics and, sometimes, Jim Barritt.

On one occasion, Joe gave a hint of another form of Barritt's perversity.

'I'm rather concerned about Jim and the way he takes statements from young girls on carnal knowledge and other sex offence matters,' he told me, his brow furrowing. 'The statements are unnecessarily explicit. It makes me wonder what his reasoning is because I haven't struck this before.'

'Anyone he interviews, he takes them into his office and closes the door. Men, women, children,' I said. 'He's so bloody secretive.'

It was a foolish practice for any copper to interview women and girls without another police officer being present, especially while investigating matters of a sexual nature. It left the interviewing officer open to all manner of claims and, of course, there remained the suggestion that he might be compromising the investigation. But Barritt did it all the time.

I never attended an interview with him—not with girls, women or men. On a number of occasions, I saw him escort a young girl into his office and close the door behind her. It had always troubled me. The girls would always leave his office distraught. That was understandable. These matters were very often traumatic for them.

I didn't go looking for carnal knowledge offences; they came to me. That's how it worked. They were often long and unpleasant investigations. But I kept them to myself. Trippy and I had learnt to go as far as we could with an investigation without involving Barritt in any way. But Barritt stood over the uniform boys, and whenever a complaint of this type was received, he'd grab it and run with it.

'The statements received from the girls don't need to go into this detail. It's lurid,' Hayes said. 'Sex acts so explicitly detailed from young girl complainants . . . it makes me wonder what he's up to.'

I took a gulp of my wine. 'Trippy and I found some photographs in his drawer.'

I did not want to tell Joe how we'd got hold of a key. It wasn't strictly honour bright.

'Photos of kids. Young girls. Maybe 10 years of age. Stark bollocking naked.'

'How many photos?'

'Four or five,' I replied.

Joe remained silent for some time.

'That doesn't surprise me. Not by the way he takes statements from teenage girls. There's something quite unusual about that man. You'd better keep an eye on this bloke, Dinny.'

There was nothing I could do about the photos. Trippy and I had virtually broken into Barritt's desk drawer to find them. If it all came out, Barritt would have offered some improbable explanation to the powers that be and he would have been believed. We would have ended up in deeper shit than him.

❖

In August 1966, 260 of Mildura's wealthiest and most influential people assembled for a formal dinner in the church parish hall. Ninety per cent of those who sat down to dinner were Catholics. I didn't get a look in; my invitation must have been lost in the mail.

There was cause for celebration. Father John Michael Joseph Day—parish priest, thief, empire builder, bricklayer for the Roman Catholic Church and prolific paedophile—was being promoted to dean.

Among the 260 VIPs toasting Day's rise up the ecclesiastical ladder was the Chief Commissioner of Police, Rupert Henry Arnold, whom his police colleagues called 'Ram's Head'—he was an unattractive man who possessed facial characteristics that were more sheep-like than human. He may as well have been called the Hurricane Lamp—dim and had to be carried.

During Arnold's seven years as chief commissioner, senior elements of the police were masterminding extortion rackets, virtually running the illegal abortion industry in Melbourne. The Kaye Abortion Inquiry of 1970 nailed some big names in the force, and three received long jail sentences—the chief of the Homicide Squad, Inspector Jack Ford; the head of the Traffic Branch, Superintendent Jack Mathews; and their bagman, Detective Constable Marty Jacobson. All their crimes had been committed under Arnold's watch.

Arnold wouldn't have had a clue. He was too busy wagging a finger at the general populace about the scourge of juvenile crime, an obsession of his. When he got to his feet at Day's celebratory dinner, he rambled on in a speech entitled, 'Juvenile delinquency—its causes and curses', summoning up spurious facts and figures that had those polishing off their chicken dinners jumping at shadows for the rest of their lives.

Chief Commissioner Rupert Arnold was a droplet of 'them' in a sea of 'us'. I'd been told he was a Freemason. No surprises there. It was a virtual prerequisite for the top job.

Arnold had worked with Barritt in the Wireless Patrol in the late 1940s. They were good friends. It was largely through Barritt's entreaties that such an esteemed member of the community had come all the way from Melbourne to speak to this august group. Barritt must have loved the cut of Arnold's jib. He'd been running around Mildura locking up drunks and harassing kids. He even arrested and charged the president of the organising committee for the local kindergarten for holding a fund-raising raffle without a licence. But if he had to investigate any serious crime, Barritt was totally out of his depth.

Joe Kearney, embezzler and rapist, was there, too, flicking his cigarette ash on to his dinner plate to adhere to the remnants of gravy he couldn't wipe up with a slice of bread. He didn't give a bugger about juvenile crime. He sloshed his whisky down before grabbing the eye of one of the children from St Joseph's who acted as unpaid waiters.

Bishop O'Collins had performed the service that moved Day one step closer to St Peter's chair. O'Collins had known of Day's paedophilia when Day was a priest in Apollo Bay, Beech Forest, Horsham and Ararat. When people complained O'Collins simply moved Day on to a new parish and let him loose on an unsuspecting community.

And in Mildura Day was monstering kids with impunity and being promoted for it. None of the 260 citizens at the dinner knew the depths of the evil going on in their town. These dark secrets belonged with Day and were vigorously suppressed by his protectors, Barritt and Kearney. Day's crimes were concealed under O'Collins's stiff, four-cornered hat, the biretta, too. They compounded Day's manifest felonies, his perverse sex crimes against children. O'Collins was an accessory before and after the fact.

The kids of Mildura might have been troubled. There were some who got into a bit of minor crime. Kids will be kids, and every country town has a group of young troublemakers. Some of the young ones eventually settle down while the others will move on to more serious crimes if they're not pulled up.

There was a group of blokes like that in Mildura—a dozen or so blokes in their late teens and early twenties. They would knock off anything that wasn't bolted to the floor. They might get into a bit of mischief at the pubs, get into a few fights, tear-arse around the streets in their cars. Like I say, every country town has them.

I knew them all. Any sort of detective worth his salt would make a point of being on speaking terms with them. They weren't fizzes or informers as such but they might give me some information every now and then, inadvertently more often than not. Most of what they told me was bullshit, but there was that little bit left over that was worth listening to. This mob of young blokes had similar résumés. They hated Barritt with a passion. That was understandable. Barritt must have booted a few up the arse at some stage, or locked them up for public drunkenness.

This mob of local louts had one thing in common. They had all attended Sacred Heart Primary School when they were kids. Some had gone on to St Joseph's College, while others had moved to the local high school. All had left school at a young age. One of them was John, known to be willing in a blue, but I got on well with him. As for the others, if I saw them out on the streets, I'd always stop them and have a yarn. They were of an age where they were a bit lost—caught in the nether world between adolescence and adulthood. Every single one of them hated John Day in a tangible, visceral fashion. Barritt I could understand, but why did they despise Day so much?

❖

In 1967 Michael was in first form at St Joseph's. Every year the school put on a play. Even at such an early age, he had an aptitude for drama and the arts, and he was cast as Oliver in the play adapted from the Charles Dickens novel *Oliver Twist*.

For weeks before the first performance, Michael wandered around at home with the script in his hand, practising his lines. In the lounge room, Jean and I gave him his prompts before he'd recite his lines. By the time the play went into full dress rehearsal, he had his lines down pat. There was an air of great excitement around our home before opening night. Michael was nervous but he was ready.

I drove him down to St Joseph's parish hall early, with Gavin sitting in the back. The play wasn't due to start for an hour or so.

When we arrived, Michael took off to get himself kitted up for his first major performance. Gavin and I took a seat in the middle of the hall. There was just a sprinkling of people in the seats—parents and siblings of the performers like Gavin and me. We had a while to wait before the play started. I looked around as the audience began to arrive, craning my neck.

I turned all the way around to the very back of the hall and saw Kearney, Barritt and Day perched up on a long bench a few steps off the ground. They must have thought they were the best seats in the house, elevated above the rest of the seating in the hall.

'Oh God,' I thought and turned straight back, hoping they hadn't spotted me.

No such luck. Within minutes, I felt a tap on the shoulder and looked around to see Joe Kearney grinning back at me.

'Dinny, you and your boy come up the back here with us,' Kearney said.

'We're right here, thanks, Joe.'

'Come on, Dinny. Take your boy up the back and he'll be able to see everything better,' Kearney insisted.

I only got up because I didn't want to cause a scene. I grabbed Gavin and followed Kearney to the back of the hall.

'Evening, Father. G'day, Jim,' I said, trying to disguise my reluctance at being among them. Barritt nodded and grunted in my general direction.

'Good evening,' Day replied. He hadn't brought himself to utter my name since we'd had the stand-up blue in the presbytery five years earlier.

Kearney went along and sat beside Barritt. I sat beside Gavin, who was wedged between me and Day.

I was still shifting in my seat, getting comfortable, when I looked down and saw that Day had firmly clasped Gavin's left hand in his. Although I knew Day was a reprobate, I had no idea of his perverse affection for children, but alarm bells were ringing at the sight of him smiling benignly while he held my boy's hand. There was something innately unnatural about it. I didn't know what. I just wanted it to stop. I got up and shifted along between Day and Gavin, then grabbed Day's wrist firmly and pulled his hand away from my son's.

'Come and sit on the other side of me, Gavin,' I said, gently directing him down along the bench away from Day. I locked eyes with Day. He stared back for a moment and gave a sickly smirk before turning away.

I took the seat alongside Day. Funnily enough, he didn't want to hold my hand.

The play finally got underway not long afterwards. The five of us sat in silence throughout the performance. Michael did a great job. I was very proud of him. If he fluffed a line I didn't notice.

At the interval Day, Kearney and Barritt got up and walked off. They didn't utter a word in our direction. I watched them make their way out of the hall. Gavin and I enjoyed the second half of the play a lot more once those bastards had gone.

The more active Catholics in Mildura were aware of the strong association between Day, Kearney and Barritt. It had caused some consternation.

❖

By mid-1965, Jean and I had had enough of the old Housing Commission home we were living in—stinking hot in summer, freezing in winter. I'd purchased a two-hectare block in Morquong, just over the river, and planned to build on it.

Ken Wright was a local real estate agent I had become friendly with. He went on to become a mayor of Mildura, then springboarded into the Victorian parliament. He was a National Party man and a good fellow. He told me that a property his parents had lived on was up for sale—six and a half hectares of mainly Valencia trees with the odd grapefruit tree, about twelve kilometres out of town on the way to Red Cliffs.

Ken explained that the farm was not a going concern. I'd struggle to turn a dollar on it. The Valencia trees produced small fruit—not really good for anything but juicing. More out of curiosity than anything else, Jean and I went to take a look at it.

We both fell in love with it straight away. We didn't love the farm so much, as we knew it would barely give us a quid and might cost us a few. But the farmhouse—a sturdy old weatherboard that had been daubed in pale blue conite, with three bedrooms, a big farm kitchen and a verandah that swept around the back and front—was a perfect family home.

I sold my block at Morquong, took a loan out with the E.S. & A. Bank and plonked down $27,000 in the brand new decimal currency.

We moved to the farm in March 1966.

As Ken had warned, the new place wasn't worth a burnt crumpet as a commercial farm, but it didn't take up a lot of my time. Contractors came in and sprayed once a year, and another contracting company looked after the picking.

After a year of living on the property, I did the accounts and discovered that I'd made the princely sum of $1000 from the farm, about twenty dollars a week, enough to pay for the weekly groceries but not much else. I told Barritt about the move. I didn't need his approval. The farm was not a business and I wasn't breaking any regulations by owning it. I just thought I'd keep him in the loop.

'I've got to have somewhere decent to live Jim,' I told him, explaining why I was moving to Red Cliffs.

Barritt just grunted. He made no suggestion that I was moonlighting on the farm. But he did have one request.

'Whenever those bludging bastards come up from Melbourne, you make sure you fill their cars up with oranges.'

Barritt was referring to the district detective inspector (DDI) and other police VIPs who might travel to Mildura from time to time.

One of the inspectors at the time was Frank Holland. Frank and I went back to the days when we'd get on the drink at O'Connor's in Melbourne. He'd taken a step or two up the ladder since Fred Russell had asked me to join the Catholic Mafia. Like Fred, Frank was a made man in the Catholic Mafia, a former inspector in Homicide and a senior in the Consorters.

Frank was the banner carrier at the St Patrick's Day march that wound its way through the Melbourne CBD, proudly singing Irish patriotic songs, like the angry, activist tune, 'The Wearing of the Green': 'Where the cruel cross of England shall nevermore be seen, and where, please God, we'll live and die still wearing of the green!'

Every time Frank left Mildura, he left with a boot heaving with oranges and grapefruit. I didn't mind this. They weren't worth anything to me and it was a good idea to keep the DDI sweet.

There were others. Eric Teese was another DDI who left Mildura with a boot-load of citrus fruits courtesy of my orchard. Another one was John 'Baton Jack' O'Connor, who eventually rose to the rank of assistant commissioner in the force.

Our new home was only two kilometres from the township of Red Cliffs. We started going to mass at St Joseph's Church at Red Cliffs. I'd still attend the Mildura church from time to time, but I saw less of Day after the move.

Michael went to St Joseph's College in Mildura, while the younger boys were at the Red Cliffs Catholic Primary School, an easy two-kilometre bike ride from home.

After we settled in, I laid a cricket pitch in the backyard. I poured the concrete and laid some malthoid over the top of it, then strung some chicken wire around it. There'd often be five or ten boys having a net with my boys and I'd give them a few tips on the finer points of the game.

I had played a couple of seasons with Mildura Manchester Unity Cricket Club when I first arrived in Mildura. It didn't take me long to find a team. I was signed up the day I got to Mildura. Trippy had let it be known that I could play a bit, so the secretary of the club had popped around the day I got to Mildura to get my signature.

So I needed Saturday afternoons off. I asked Barritt if he could swing it for me.

'No worries,' he said in a brief moment of helpfulness before he paused. 'You are playing with Sacred Heart, I presume?'

'No, I'm playing with Mildura MU.'

'Well, you won't be getting your Saturday afternoons off then,' Barritt pronounced and strode off to his office.

Bugger that and bugger him, I thought. I took my Saturday afternoons off in the cricket season. There were just the three of us in CIB anyway, including Barritt, and he was as useful as an ashtray on a motorbike. Playing cricket didn't mean I was away from the to and fro of police work.

I remember being halfway through an over when the police van pulled up and a couple of uniform officers walked onto the field to tell me there had been a shooting. I bowled the last couple of balls, took my hat from the umpire and that was me gone for the rest of the day.

Police work in a country town was like that. You couldn't be sure what would happen at any given time. One minute all was quiet, save for a few outstanding minor matters. The next thing I'd be investigating a murder.

A week or so before Christmas in 1966, I was in the CIB office and took a call from Jack Thomas, one of the uniform policemen at Merbein. He told me he had some information that a murder had been committed.

I told Barritt what Thomas had told me. He was immediately dismissive.

'Thomas doesn't know what he's talking about. He wouldn't know if a tram was up him. And he's a bloody Mason.'

'Look, Jim,' I told him while grabbing the keys to the CIB car, 'I'm going over there anyway.'

Thomas took me out to the banks of the river at Cowanna Bend just outside Merbein. I saw tyre tracks leading to the edge of a drop of three or four metres. A huge chunk of the embankment had been carved out. I interviewed a woman who lived in a shanty about forty metres away. She confirmed what Thomas had told me. She had seen two people, a man and a woman, push a station wagon into the river at dusk the day before.

I went back to Merbein and rang the Search and Rescue Squad in Melbourne. That was not strictly my call. Police procedures dictated that only an inspector or someone higher up the ladder could make a decision like that. The Search and Rescue boys didn't seem to mind and said they would be there the following day.

I went back to the office and rang the head of Homicide, Frank Holland, my old mate and the recipient of a good portion of the fruits of my orchard. I told him that I'd called in the Search and Rescue boys to drag the river.

'Dinny, you've broken every rule in the book,' Frank told me. 'I'll back you but you'd better bloody well be right on this. I'll send two of our blokes up. They'll be there early in the morning. Put me on to Jim.'

While Holland was on the phone to Barritt, I took the opportunity to ring the Wentworth police station across the river in New South Wales. The jurisdictional vagaries needed to be sorted. New South Wales owns the river. Victoria owns only its southern banks. If the murder had taken place in the river, it would have been a matter for the New South Wales police force. The officer at Wentworth told me there'd be two detectives and a forensic team brought down from Broken Hill to assist in the investigation and maybe take it over if it turned out to be one of theirs.

By the time I got off the phone teeing all that up, Barritt was standing in front of me.

'You'd better know what you're talking about this time,' he warned before marching back to his office. 'If you bugger this up, you'll be in more muck than a Werribee duck.'

The following morning, Search and Rescue had their scuba team in the water. The two detectives from New South Wales rowed a four-metre boat out on the river, while the scuba divers rummaged around below in the silty brown water.

Like a cork in a bottle, a bleached, bloated body bobbed up to the surface next to the little rowboat. The two detectives nearly shat themselves. Hydrogen sulphide, carbon dioxide and methane, produced in the body after death, had swelled the corpse to almost twice its usual size. The divers had found the station wagon on the bottom of the river, then levered the tailgate open, and the body had rushed out as if keen to escape its murky wet grave.

The body was brought onto the riverbank further downstream, where Jack Thomas identified it as Illario Geracitano, a local market gardener. Geracitano had a long history of mental illness and was known to the Merbein police as a man who had been violent towards his wife and son on numerous occasions.

I had done some training as a police photographer so I drew the short straw and grabbed an old Rolleicord camera out of the car, took a deep breath and took some snaps of the body before getting away from the stench as fast as I could.

I had taken just long enough over the body to see that Geracitano's hands and feet had been bound. I snapped away at the ligatures. There was a small hole in the centre of his head. I photographed this, too. It may have been a gunshot wound. I couldn't be sure. That was something that would be examined during the post-mortem.

The following day, the headlines in the Melbourne papers screamed that Geracitano had been shot in the head. Barritt was quoted at length, saying Geracitano had been shot, a big call prior to the post-mortem, although he'd had bugger all to do with the case at that time. He was big-noting again.

It turned out that Barritt was way off the mark. Geracitano hadn't been shot. The autopsy report revealed that Geracitano had been beaten to death with a blunt object. The hole in his forehead had occurred after death. Geracitano's head injuries had been so significant, and his skull had been fractured so many times, that gases had built up in his head to a point where the pressure had blown a hole through the skin.

It wasn't just the circumstances of Geracitano's death that Barritt had got wrong. He thought he knew who'd committed the murder, too. Not specifically, of course. He didn't have a name or a face. Barritt, in full J. Edgar Hoover mode, became convinced that the murder was a Mafia contract killing, no doubt committed by a hit man with a violin case and perhaps a scar across his cheek from some youthful street brawl.

The following day, Barritt took one of the Homicide Squad detectives, Sergeant Noel Murphy, out on a crusade. Barritt hit all his fizzes in the Italian community, demanding information. From there, he barged into the homes, farms and factories in and outside Mildura, targeting the Italians he suspected were Mafia men.

These poor blokes were bailed up against walls and read the riot act by Barritt. He was on to them, he said. Their day of reckoning was at hand. It would be better for them to fess up and throw themselves on the mercy of the courts. They had nothing to tell him, of course. Rather than acknowledge that he was climbing up the wrong tree, Barritt took their stunned faces as a sure sign that the Mafia's reach was greater than even he had suspected. 'Omerta' was the problem, but he, and only he, would break down the code of silence.

Meanwhile, I took the other homicide officer, Detective Senior Constable John Bates, out to Geracitano's home. His widow, Teresa, wasn't home but their 17-year-old son was. We took him back to the station and interviewed him. Within ten minutes he broke down and confessed that he and his mother had killed his father. The old man had had one of his violent rages and as usual had taken it out on the boy and his mother. The three had wrestled each other to the ground, and Teresa had grabbed a block of firewood and bounced it off her husband's head a few times. Teresa and the boy hadn't been sure their tormentor was dead, so they bound his hands and feet, put him in the old station wagon and pushed it into the drink at Cowanna Bend.

Later that day I had a beer with Noel Murphy and John Bates. I had to ask.

'How was your day?' I asked Noel.

'What a fucking embarrassment that bastard Barritt is,' Noel replied. 'He dragged me all over Mildura looking for the bloody Mafia. He was banging on doors and threatening people all day with murder blues. Jesus, the poor buggers didn't have a clue what was going on.'

Bates and I couldn't stop laughing. Noel had copped Barritt in full flight. I was just glad it was someone else on the receiving end for a change.

'There's something very, very wrong with that man,' Noel said, downing his beer.

On another occasion, Barritt let a murderer walk free. It wasn't corruption. Not in the traditional sense. It was a matter of sheer investigative ineptitude, tinged with Barritt's view that ethnic families should not be afforded the same investigative rigour as good Anglo-Saxon families in the area.

Barritt had a strong association with a prominent Croatian family in Mildura. He was using one of the family members to get information for his reports to ASIO. The Croats were the good guys in the post-war period and the Serbs the objects of suspicion—the reds under the beds in Mildura. Barritt would thump out his reports based on some scurrilous piece of information he'd picked up around the traps.

This particular family operated an illegal still and made its own grappa. They sold a few bottles on the sly to their former countrymen around Mildura and drank the rest. They were known to be heavy drinkers, guzzling away on the almost pure spirit of the home-made grog.

The mother of this Croatian family was elderly, in her eighties, but still spritely, and she could belt down the grappa as well as men half her age.

One day she was found dead in her home wearing her nightgown. A lounge room window had been forced open and a television set next to the window had been knocked over. Despite evidence pointing to a murder and aggravated burglary, Barritt decided the woman had died of natural causes. He didn't bother with the burglary either. He didn't demand a post-mortem, so there was none. A death certificate was hastily issued and that was that.

I found this out only two years later when a fizz told me he'd been at the house the night the woman died. He told me he had been part of a group of five pickers who'd been out drinking at the bottom bar of the Wintersun Hotel in town, pissing their money up against a wall. One of the group told the others that he knew of a house nearby where an old lady lived. The son was never home. He'd just break in and knock off some money.

The informer told me that this bloke did break in, jemmied the window open while the rest of the group looked on. So drunk was he that the moment his foot was on the floor, he knocked over the television set. The old lady was roused from her slumber and made her way down to the lounge room to see what the racket was. She saw the bloke and screamed. He grabbed the woman, threw her to the ground and suffocated her by holding the palm of his hand over her mouth while pinching her nostrils shut.

He came out of the house a few moments later.

'She won't be screaming anymore,' he told the group.

In the end we hunted down the witnesses, who by then had spread all over the country, before arresting the murderer, Mustafa Kulenovic. As Barritt had buggered the initial investigation, there was no medical evidence to prove a cause of death. There was no point in exhuming the body. Too much time had elapsed since the woman had been murdered.

The best we could do was charge him with aggravated burglary. Kulenovic pleaded guilty and got ten years.

When I told Barritt what the informer had told me, he denied any involvement in the first investigation, but he could not sustain it. The records were there for all to see.

I'd learnt to keep my distance with Barritt but on this occasion I couldn't help myself.

'Jim, what were you thinking?' I said, more incredulous than anything. 'This was a stone cold break and enter gone wrong.'

'You don't know what you're talking about. Bloody piss-pot wog. She just fell over. Bloody pizzles.'

Of course, Barritt might have thought, what's two bungled murder investigations when three will do?

The Stock Squad detective from Deniliquin, a town in New South Wales about 400 kilometres east of Mildura, regularly paid us a visit. Early in 1965, he called in with news of a murder up Forbes way. A young farm labourer had grabbed a shotgun, shot the farmer's wife dead and stolen some cash from the property. He gave us a circular with the labourer's description, so we pinned it up on the noticeboard at the CIB office and at the front of the station for the uniform boys.

One morning I was sitting in the CIB office. Barritt's office door was closed, and I knew he had a couple of young blokes in there with him, itinerant farm labourers in their early twenties. They'd been picked up by the uniform boys after being spotted hitchhiking in town.

'You're a pair of pooftah bastards,' Barritt thundered from his office. 'What have you been stealing, you bastards?' Bang! Crash!

The sounds of the two young men whimpering in reply confirmed that Barritt was giving them his version of the third degree. A thumping.

The interview went on for about twenty minutes, interspersed with more crashing sounds, with Barritt trying to beat a confession out of them. Finally, the door swung open and out marched the monstrous Barritt with two forlorn young blokes in tow. Not a mark on them. I had to give Barritt his due there.

'Put these two pooftahs in the interview book,' Barritt told me before he marched back to his office.

I looked over at these two young blokes. One of them was nuggety and solidly built, almost as tall as Barritt. The other was shorter, and scrawny but muscular and wiry. He fitted the description of the Forbes murder suspect to a tee.

I walked gingerly into Barritt's office.

'Jim,' I said, 'do you mind if I have a word with these two?'

Barritt didn't answer directly. No doubt the cogs were grinding in his suet pudding of a mind.

'All right. But you won't get anything out of them.' Barritt clearly thought that if these two blokes had survived one of his thumpings they had to be innocent.

I interviewed the taller one first. He didn't have much to say. I wrote him up in the interview book and said he could go.

The scrawny bloke was next. I asked where he'd been, and he told me he'd been a jackaroo all over New South Wales and Victoria. I told him I'd been a rouseabout before I'd joined the force. I'd worked at a pastoral station on the Narrandera Run almost twenty years before. He knew the property. He'd worked there.

I waited until he finished describing the station as it was when he'd worked on it, then let the silence hang.

'Why did you do it?' I asked. His head went down straight away.

'Your description is on every police noticeboard in New South Wales and Victoria. You're wanted for murder. You can't run away from this.'

The tears flowed. He looked up at me and blurted it all out. He was broke and only wanted to rob the place. He couldn't explain why he'd shot the woman. It was just a stupid and pointless crime.

I took down the details of confession and left him to ponder his fate. I walked into Barritt's office.

'Jim, one of these young blokes has just put his hand up for the murder in Forbes. You know the one? On the noticeboard.'

I was enjoying this. A good detective doesn't let details slip. I had memorised the description of the suspect. Barritt hadn't even noticed the flyer on the noticeboard and had forgotten the briefing the Deniliquin Stock Squad detective had given us less than a month before. He rose from his chair and made his way out the door. He could move quickly for a big man when he was motivated. He brushed past me, grabbed the remorseful young killer by the scruff of his neck and dragged him back into his office.

'I'll handle this!' Barritt roared, and slammed the door in my face.

He tried to take the pinch as his own. He did it routinely to advance his reputation with the senior blokes at Russell Street. He must have taken thirty or forty arrests off me over the years. He did the same with the uniform boys. Helped himself to any other arrest that caught his eye and left the officer who'd done the hard work empty-handed. That was the way Barritt was—a terrible detective who wouldn't know shit from clay if he'd eaten a mouthful of it.

I just thought he was a clod—an overgrown version of Inspector Clouseau, a bumbling fool, but with a nasty streak that he used to keep his fellow officers under his control. I didn't think he was corrupt. Not at that stage anyway. But he was worse than any copper who took a backhander to look the other way. And he was protecting Day.

Had Trippy or Mick O'Donnell told me that Barritt was standing over parents, forcing them to drop complaints that Day had raped and assaulted their children, I would have been right on to him from the outset. But it was all a deep secret. Anything that came into Mildura station involving Day went straight to Barritt. And from there the complaints would disappear, leaving kids tormented, their lives suspended in a dim purgatory.

Strangely, it didn't seem odd to me that Barritt, Day and Joe Kearney dined together at the presbytery every other day. I didn't like any of them so I kept my distance. Out of sight, out of mind. I didn't question it. I knew the three of them would be there together, boozing up. That didn't bother me. It just seemed like three strange men acting out their small-town fantasies behind closed doors.

I couldn't have been more wrong. They would fill their bellies in the presbytery, and plot and scheme. Kearney would produce the books, and Day and he would scour through them, item by item, looking for anything they could swipe. If money was short, Barritt would know what to do. There were always the local villains to shake down—the SP bookies, the sly groggers, the bludgers and anyone else Barritt could stand over.

This unholy trinity controlled Mildura. Barritt warded off or intimidated troublemakers. Kearney controlled the courts and Day, a man who purported to be chosen by God to manage all His concerns and interests on earth, would suit himself.

❖

Trippy had been driving back from Renmark along the Sturt Highway. It was a ninety-minute trip, almost two hours if you took it easy. It could be a lonely drive, especially at night. The odd truck laden with produce from Mildura might have passed him by, but for the most part Trippy was on his own, flashing past the hop bush, the native pines and the mallee gums that pockmarked the wheat and sheep farms along the highway.

Trippy fell asleep at the wheel of his old FC Holden and slammed into a mallee gum. The old car was built to take the impact, but without a seatbelt, Trippy slammed into the steering wheel. He had been stuck out there in his wreck of a car, injured and near death for close to an hour, before help arrived.

He spent a month in hospital with chest injuries. He made a full recovery but the steering wheel had bruised his heart, weakening it and making Trippy susceptible to heart failure. The accident had effectively given him a shortened use-by date.

He didn't talk about it much to me. I can't remember him even talking about the accident. Perhaps he did in passing. The uniform boys had told me how serious it had been, but even they didn't know that Trippy's heart had copped such a colossal wallop that it would take decades off his life.

Not long after the accident, Trippy took sick leave. His heart had been giving him problems again. I'd call on him at his home a couple of times a week. He was losing weight and his usual swarthy complexion was fading. He began to deteriorate before my eyes. He still managed to come into the CIB office from time to time for a chat, but his visits had become less frequent as time wore on.

One morning I looked up from my desk and there was Trippy standing in front of me. He looked terrible, like he could collapse at any time. I leapt out of my chair and encouraged him to take a seat but Trippy was having none of that.

'I need to have a word with you outside,' he said, nodding towards the old bitumen tennis court at the back of the station. I followed, keeping an eye on him as he struggled down the corridor. He stood still for a moment, looking at me carefully.

'I'm fucked,' he told me. 'I've had it. I've only got a couple of days to live.'

I was shocked. I knew he was crook but I didn't know he was this bad.

'Is there anything I can do?'

'Yes,' Trippy said. 'Keep an eye on Addy and the kids.'

'Don't worry. I'll look after them, mate.'

'Good,' he said. 'I've got to get going.'

I didn't know what to say. In the end there was nothing I *could* say and Trippy knew it. He turned and walked off slowly around to Madden Avenue. I imagine his wife, Adrianna, was there, waiting for him in the car.

It was just like Trippy. He didn't want a fuss. He was an all-round good bloke and copper. A bit of a loner, like me.

He didn't stand for any bullshit, even from mugs of higher rank like Barritt. Maybe that's why we gravitated towards each other. And here he was, at just 37 years of age, shuffling off home to wait for the executioner.

Two days later, Adrianna called me at home, just after nine o'clock in the evening. Trippy was gone. She'd been sitting on the lounge and Trippy was on his feet, standing by the mantelpiece. He just collapsed in front of her without a word. And that was that. Dead before he hit the ground.

Trippy was an atheist. He regarded the concepts of immaculate conception and the resurrection as con artistry put about by Bible bashers. He'd been a Mason, but I don't think he took that very seriously either. I don't know how often he attended lodge meetings. He didn't speak about it. He was more comfortable with a beer in his hand, having a punt on the gee-gees or holding a hot poker hand in a tough school with plenty of dough in the kitty. God only knows what Trippy would have made of the religious service in his honour at the local Anglican church, but he would have smiled at the big crowd who attended.

I led the funeral procession down Deakin Avenue behind the hearse, out in front of a dozen uniform police as the cortege wound its way to the cemetery at Nicholls Point. I kept it together at the cemetery as best I could as Trippy's coffin was lowered into the ground.

One of the local councillors, who had a big citrus orchard over the river in Curlwaa, put on a wake in his backyard with a barbecue and a barrel. There were a few civilians there and around twenty coppers—some from South Australia, some from New South Wales and the rest of us from Victoria.

Barritt didn't make an appearance. He wouldn't have been welcome anyway.

We got on the drink, shed a few tears and told a few of Trippy's stories.

5

POWER WITHOUT GLORY

The Catholic Church keeps going because it has been repeating the same thing for two thousand years.
JOSEPH GOEBBELS, 1897–1945

It was common knowledge that Monsignor John Day took children away on weekend trips. Day would drive his big, new model American car out of Mildura with a young boy, or sometimes two, sitting alongside him on the long bench seat. He'd been doing it for years.

More often than not, he'd drive the boys down to Melbourne and take them to the Melbourne Cricket Ground to watch a game of Australian Rules football. Afterwards, Day and the boys would travel on to Day's sister's house in Williamstown and spend the night there.

Day's parishioners were full of praise. What a man! What a priest, to devote so much of his time to the service of the children in his flock. More acclaim was extended to Day when he drove down the Calder Highway to Melbourne with a group of girls from Sacred Heart Primary School to see the hit musical *The Sound of Music*.

Day taught physical education lessons to the boys in grades five and six at Sacred Heart. The PE classes often involved gymnastics training, where the boys would launch off a springboard and vault a pommel horse onto a mat while Day looked on.

Day would hold competitions to see who could vault the best. The prize for the winners was a trip to Melbourne or to some other part of Victoria where Day had business. Sometimes Day and the boys would stay in motels but, when in Melbourne, they always found themselves at his sister's Williamstown home.

The boys not singled out for their vaulting skills may still have found themselves under Day's control as altar boys.

In the Catholic community, being an altar boy could add considerable prestige to a boy's family. Hands would shoot up in the Sacred Heart classrooms when the nuns asked for volunteers. The sisters would screen a few of the more mischievous boys out and the remaining dozen or so would be marched across to Day in the church for his approval. The selection process would often come down to who the prospective altar boys' parents were. The more devout the parents were, the more trusting they would be about leaving their children in Day's company.

If selected, the boys would go home to inform their parents, who would beam with pride. It meant the family's status in the parish had gone up a notch.

In any year, eight or ten altar boys were chosen to perform duties in the church under the supervision of Day, usually in groups of two or three according to a roster prepared by Day. Their duties included laying out prayer books along the pews, lighting candles and helping him prepare for mass and holy communion.

In those days there were four masses on Sundays: at 7 am, 8 am and 10 am, and one evening mass at 5 pm. Every other day of the week there would be just one mass at 7 am.

Some of the altar boys would be at the Mildura church, alone with Day, for hours on end.

Other children, who had missed out on Day's favour, would be approached to perform tasks around the church. It might be sweeping the tennis court or washing his big American car. Day would often give them money for their efforts.

Over the years Day had carefully contrived to be alone with hundreds of boys and girls in Mildura. And he frequently visited the other parishes in the diocese where he had what he referred to as 'his boys'—victims he had forced into submission by threatening to have them sent to boys' homes.

Outwardly, he was a pillar of the community, trusted and respected by his parishioners. It was a carefully planned and executed piece of deception. Day had been raping children for years, but he knew how to keep the kids quiet and the parents ignorant or incapable of believing his debauchery.

I knew nothing of this at the time. He was a cautious, calculating man and his authority in the community was absolute. Not even a whisper of his crimes fell on my ears. If there were rumours, they were muttered surreptitiously. And if one parent did look like making a noise, Barritt came to Day's rescue.

Joe Kearney and Day were also busy perusing the accounts. Money was piling into the church building fund. The old Mildura Church, moved en masse from Lime Avenue to its ultimate home in Eleventh Street in 1922, had outlived its usefulness. It would ultimately be transformed into a red-brick edifice twice its size, largely to help Day's promotion up the ecclesiastical step ladder.

I knew one of the builders who tendered for the job. Terry Lynch worked for S. J. Weir, a construction company based in Ballarat. Terry was a Catholic and at one point had been a member of Day's inner circle. I guess he thought he had a rails run for the job but he soon discovered Day was a miser with other people's money.

Time and time again Terry trudged into the presbytery with the church renovation and extension plans under his arm. Each time Day would peruse the plans and demand cuts to the bottom line.

The money was in the bank. The Church Building Fund was swollen to bursting point with parishioners' donations. Day's penny-pinching did not save the parishioners a few bob here and there.

He wanted to pocket any money left over. Those big American cars he drove didn't come cheap.

In the end Terry threw up his hands and walked away from the job.

A local builder, John Blain, won the contract. God only knows what hoops Day made Blain jump through to get it.

And while this madness went on, the church building fund kept ticking over. It became a vast repository of funds, thanks to the generosity of Mildura's Catholics and the fraud that Day and Kearney had cooked up.

Day's sermons, often characterised by outrage and a great wringing of hands over the decline of moral standards in young people, would invariably end with demands for more and more money for the building fund. The collection plate went around the church twice at each mass. The morning mass at ten o'clock each Sunday would have the old church full and fit to burst—standing room only down the back. Parishioners would flip their hard-earned into the plate, often under Jim Barritt's watchful eye. It didn't end there. After mass, we'd all walk out of the church, past a stall where religious bric-a-brac and spiritual paraphernalia were on sale—crosses, Bibles, rosary beads, prayer cards. You name it, Day would make a quid out of it.

And then there was the mid-week envelope, often delivered to parishioners' homes by schoolchildren on the walk home from school. It came attached to a begging letter from Day. Others went out in the mail. Parishioners' wallets and purses were under constant assault.

Money was obtained by fair means and foul. Kearney, the treasurer, didn't mind where it came from. If the money was black, the light of the Church would render it clean.

John Lavarnos was a businessman who ran a coffee shop in Deakin Avenue which doubled as an illegal gaming house. There were no roulette wheels or poker machines. The big money changed hands at the card tables. Lavarnos was a pimp, too, and the gamblers could curtail their betting to spend some time with the prostitutes he had walking the floor.

I knew all about what was going on in Deakin Avenue within a few weeks of arriving in Mildura. Trippy had pulled me up and told me that Barritt protected Lavarnos, and the club was hands off to all other police officers.

I could have gone down and knocked the place over any time but if I did, Barritt would have turned my life upside down with dodgy complaints and disciplinary charges. I knew that. I didn't want the big oaf all over me. I wasn't interested in sly groggers or gaming anyway. I was trained to catch serious crooks. Barritt could have the bookies, card sharks and pimps. This was the division of labour Barritt had established with other detectives, and he had the uniform boys bluffed so that any complaint about gaming or sly grogging went straight to him anyway.

The Sacred Heart Peace Memorial Church was due to open its doors in 1969. But what great edifice to the glory of God would be complete without a brand new church organ? The old organ was fine. It could have been wheeled into the new church, but Day was having none of that. He put the word out to his trusted lieutenants, Barritt and Kearney, that a new organ was needed. God would not provide. Some big money was needed from a suitable donor in the earthly dimension.

Police reservist Bill Brodie pulled me aside in the CIB office early one Monday morning. As a reservist, Bill was a sort of clerk around the CIB office, helping out with paperwork. He'd retired from the force after thirty years' service. A big man in his late fifties, he'd been a police champion heavyweight boxer and had played football for North Melbourne in the Victorian Football League. Barritt had brought him into the office to act as a bulwark between himself and me.

It didn't work out that way. Bill may have been a devout Catholic and a tireless worker for the parish, but he didn't much care for Barritt and, in his policeman's way, he knew what Barritt was up to and pretended not to notice. Bill wouldn't play Barritt's game. He was too smart for that. He got on with his duties at the police station and kept out of the politics.

I'd been going to mass at Red Cliffs. I wasn't up to date with the parish chatter in Mildura. I knew the new church was due to open but that was about it.

'Do you want to hear something funny?' Bill asked, with a mug of tea in his hand. He had a mischievous grin on his face and that told me I wanted to hear more.

'Throughout the service everyone was admiring the new church organ. Brand spanking new. Wonderful sound it makes. Must have cost four large at least,' Bill said, his grin growing wider.

'Then Day got up and thanked the Holy Name Sodality for our efforts in raising the money to buy the new organ. I'm on the committee. We don't have two bob to rub together. Johnny Lavarnos paid for that organ. You know how close Jim is to Lavarnos,' Bill said, as he walked off, laughing.

Lavarnos was no Catholic. He was a man with a distant relationship to God at best. But he had paid for the new organ. It was the cost of doing business in Mildura. Barritt had encouraged Lavarnos to be more community minded. It must have come as a shock. Barritt's usual backhander from Lavarnos—probably fifty dollars a week to look the other way—was suddenly jacked up to $3000 out of the blue.

Day wanted a new organ for his new church. No worries. Barritt would get the dough.

Lavarnos made a fortune out of his club but his surreptitious donation to the church would have emptied his wallet.

Three grand was a lot of dough in 1969. He never did get to listen to the organ he paid for.

Barritt also stood over every SP bookmaker in town. They knew the cost of doing business, too. It was either a backhander or mail to Barritt, but usually both. One bookie had a particularly strange demand made of him.

'Monsignor Day will have ten quid on the winner of the last race,' Barritt told him.

The SP knew exactly what that meant.

It wasn't gambling. It was a sure thing. Whichever horse won the last race, Day would win whatever it paid. If it was an even money favourite, Day pocketed twenty dollars, but if a roughie got up in the get out of jail stakes, he would walk away with two or three hundred.

The arrangement had been going on for years before the church was built. Some of the SP's dough was going into the building fund. Some of it went straight into Day's back pocket, depending on how Kearney viewed the accounts.

Barritt was a one-man extortion racket, while Day and Kearney were scrambling for the money to get the church built.

A couple of interstate truckers living in Mildura who liked to fish in the Murray decided to go halves and buy a tinny. They agreed that one would buy the boat, the other the outboard motor, figuring that was more or less a fifty-fifty deal.

The trucker whose responsibility it was to buy the motor bought one that had fallen off the back of a truck, so to speak. He'd been unloading his truck at a depot in Footscray and a Flash Harry had offered him a deal on an outboard motor—a third off the retail price. The trucker must have known it was hot but he only told his mate that he had picked up a bargain. The trucker who'd purchased the tinny itself didn't have a clue so when he took the motor in for repairs to the local shop, the motor came up stolen and the police were called in.

Barritt took charge of the investigation. The trucker who had bought the hot motor was dragged into the station. He was told he'd be charged for receiving. The trucker was aghast. He could lose his job over this. Was there nothing that could be done?

As it turned out, there was. The church building fund was in need of cash. If the trucker agreed to put some money in—a couple of grand in today's money—Barritt could guarantee he would avoid a conviction. It seemed like a pretty sweet deal to the trucker. He made a statement acknowledging that he had realised the motor was hot when he bought it.

Meanwhile, Barritt headed out to the trucker's mate's place and started heavying him. The motor was stolen and he too would be charged, Barritt told him. The poor bloke was innocent, but that didn't matter. Barritt ordered him to report to the police station to make a statement. The bloke maintained his innocence, so Barritt told him to go home and stay there while the investigation continued.

The following morning, the guilty trucker appeared at Mildura Court bright and early. The clerk of the courts, Kearney, made sure the trucker came up first before the magistrate, Joe Hayes, and on the basis of a glowing character reference from Barritt, the man was given a six-month good behaviour bond. At Barritt's request he was required to attend the police station on his way home. The fellow was relieved that he had avoided a conviction and thanked Barritt for his kind words in the court.

'You don't have to thank me,' Barritt said. 'Make a donation to the church building fund. And make it a big one.'

The abashed trucker babbled out that he would do as he was told.

'And your mate,' Barritt growled. 'He has to put his hand in his pocket for the building fund, too.'

The two truckers met later that day. They knew they were being extorted and they weren't happy about it. They knew also that Barritt would make life unbearable for them if they didn't pony up to Monsignor John Day's building fund. Barritt would put them on the hit list with the mobile traffic boys, and they'd be pulled over every time they drove down the highway. Reluctantly, they got out their cheque books. They paid a hundred dollars each in cheques made payable to the Sacred Heart building fund and dropped them off directly at the church.

That was just one rort. I only found out about it later, when there was an investigation into Barritt. There wasn't an SP bookie or sly grogger in Mildura that Barritt hadn't shaken down for money to build this new edifice for the glory of God.

Barritt had no visible signs of wealth, no opulent cars or other affectations of the wealthy. He had no children and lived comfortably in a modest house. He was a punter and a big one, but the way he stood over the SPs around town meant he was betting with their money, not his.

The money went straight into the hands of Kearney and Day. Day did have expensive habits. Big cars. Fine wines. And most expensive of all, his building projects.

It is a dirty little secret not much talked about by the people of Mildura. The Sacred Heart Peace Memorial Church, consecrated in August 1969, owed its existence at least in part to dirty money, corruptly obtained. From the church organ to the very bricks and mortar, black money built and furnished this edifice to the glory of God.

❖

Day's promotion to dean in 1967 enhanced his authority in the Mildura parish, and his power grew beyond it. As dean he had the right to examine all Church records within his own parish as well as a number of neighbouring parishes within the Ballarat diocese. He had additional pastoral duties to all priests within the diocese and was responsible for their well-being, both spiritual and mortal.

Day was a lover of pageantry and costume, the trappings of the Church. He wore the black cassock of a priest, the black signifying death and resurrection; the collar, a sign of obedience; the sash or cincture around his waist, a sign of his chastity. At the big Italian weddings in Mildura, Day was resplendent in his white vestments, which he also wore on Christmas and Easter Sunday and for christenings. Come Advent and Lent, Day was decked out in purple. On Good Friday it was red to signify the blood of Christ. On any ordinary Sunday not combined with some church festival, Day would stand proudly, dressed in his emerald green vestments.

He was always immaculately attired and his vestments were redolent of dry-cleaning fluids. He always looked like he'd just stepped out of a glass case in some liturgical museum. Day observed the pomp and ceremony of the Church more than other priests. It was part of his conceit, standing in front of the congregation as if he was their monarch, their ruler, their tyrant.

The vestments and the ceremonies are deeply arcane, immersed in the rituals of the Church. The intricacies are beyond the understanding of most Catholics, including me. So how could it be that I found myself wearing Day's vestments? It is some sort of rich irony that would see me wearing Father Day's priestly clothes in public.

Like most parents, Jean and I became a taxi service on weekends. The boys played badminton, table tennis and soccer. Michael and Martin played cricket. Gavin played basketball. Anthony was into weightlifting.

They were all strong swimmers. Michael and Martin, who also suffered from asthma, started swimming, as we were told it was a good activity for asthmatics. Michael became the captain of the swimming team at Red Cliffs. Their health improved through swimming, and their asthma attacks became less frequent. The doctors in Mildura still cautioned me that neither Michael nor Martin was cleared of asthma. A shift to a different climate, especially one that didn't afford a welter of sports and activities like swimming, might still put them at risk.

I got to know the parents of the other kids who were training at the pool. We'd get together for a barbecue most Saturday nights. We were enjoying a meal and a few beers at the Staintons' home on one of these evenings when Gwen Stainton asked me if I was interested in getting into the thespian caper with the local theatre group, the Red Cliffs Players. I wasn't keen at first, but Gwen is a very persuasive person and before I knew it I was ready for my theatrical debut in a play called *The Young Wife*. I was terrified but Gwen and the other cast members put me at ease. We performed to a full house, and once the nerves were out of the way, I enjoyed it.

When a one-act play festival came up, the Red Cliffs Players entered a play called *A Nun's Story*. I played the bishop, the lead role. I needed a costume, but I wasn't going to go to Ballarat and knock on the Cathedral door and ask the bishop if I could borrow his. I didn't want to front the presbytery in Mildura out of the blue, either.

A few days shy of the festival, I spoke to Barritt in the office. I explained that I was playing a bishop in a play and was looking for assistance with the costume.

'He's not a bishop—yet,' Barritt replied.

'It won't matter. Ninety-nine per cent of the audience won't know the difference,' I said. 'Can you ask him?'

I didn't want to go and see Day. I was hoping Barritt would collect the clothes from Day and all I'd have to do was grab them off him at the station.

'I'll see what I can do,' Barritt said, with a smile.

But there was no dodging Day. The following day Barritt told me to call into the presbytery later that morning. Day was waiting for me outside the presbytery with his freshly dry-cleaned cassock and the biretta. Day had a grin from ear to ear when I collected them from him. He barely said a word to me and I merely muttered something about returning them to him on the following Monday.

I wore the cassock and the biretta that Saturday night. I am not too modest to say that the play was a hit with the audience. I didn't check Day's cassock for stains. I had no reason to. It was perfectly clean, superficially at least, but it was stained all right, deeply soiled by his rape of children, and by his remorseless theft and fraud.

Day was a psychopath. I have no doubt about that now. His grandiosity was the first and most obvious sign; his remorseless sexual attacks on children were another; and his unabashed theft of parishioners' money—many of whom were struggling to make ends meet—a third.

Day lived well. He always had a new car. He'd tell people that his sister had bought it for him. He was good at establishing an alibi. He used to tell people that his family had money. I found out later that his family was dirt poor. Back when he was at his first parish, Colac, he used to run the school canteen, where he helped himself to the money. When the school brought up the fact that the canteen was trading at a significant loss, he claimed that he could not bring himself to accept money from little kids for ice creams and soft drinks. It was all bullshit. Day took more than money from kids. He stole their innocence and their prospects.

He had a couple of sisters and I chased them up many years later. One sister lived in the modest Williamstown home. His other sister lived in Killarney, a little village just outside Warrnambool. I checked out the house, an old stone dwelling that looked like it had only just been hooked up to electricity. There was no money in Day's family. Every cent he had came either from the small stipend he received from the diocese or the money he stole or extorted.

He had no compunction, no capacity for empathy. And he was left to run roughshod over the people he was supposed to serve. Bishop O'Collins knew. He'd heard the complaints about Day's behaviour from parishioners. Some of the complaints had been made directly to police. Nothing was done. Day, decked out in all his religious finery, was a much-valued member of the Ballarat diocese. He brought what others could not—money. And so what if he had a predilection towards raping and assaulting children? That could all be swept away.

At worst, O'Collins would tell Day to pack his bags and move on to another parish and another unsuspecting community, where he would be free to do as he pleased. The likelihood of Day getting his marching orders from Mildura, however, was becoming more remote by the moment. Day was firmly ensconced, with the vast edifice of the new church built for the glorification of the Church. This man, this priest, this psychopath was virtually unstoppable.

While Day was raping kids, Barritt would be belting some poor bloke and dumping him bleeding on the side of the road, while Kearney was leering at and sexually assaulting young women in his office.

These were the men who ran Mildura in the 1960s, and their power was almost unlimited.

6

THE CATHOLIC MAFIA

Truth exists, only lies are invented.
GEORGES BRAQUE, 1882–1963

On 1 May 1971 James Patrick O'Collins retired as bishop of the Ballarat diocese. He had been a bishop for forty-one years, thirty of those at Ballarat.

Somewhere in a locked drawer in O'Collins's office sat *Crimen Sollicitationis*—the 1962 papal instruction on how a bishop must handle the perverse business of priests soliciting parishioners for sex—gathering dust. O'Collins knew it back to front. When a complaint was made against Ridsdale or Day or any other paedophile priest, he knew what to do. But O'Collins had been Day's protector and facilitator, and he had done the same with Father Gerald Ridsdale. Whenever the cries of outrage and violation became too loud, O'Collins simply moved the men on to new parishes where they could molest and rape a new flock of innocent children.

O'Collins lived to a fine old age. He died in 1983, just five months short of his ninety-second birthday. Bishops, like popes, often tend to live long lives. Perhaps this is due to living in comfort and splendour, never having to worry about paying the mortgage or the rent. Perhaps, too, the good Lord isn't eager for them to join him.

O'Collins was replaced by Ronald Austin Mulkearns. Ordained a bishop in 1968, Mulkearns was given the title of Bishop of Cululi, a now defunct diocese in Tunisia. He had no diocesan authority; it was an appointment in name only. Essentially Mulkearns remained in Ballarat as coadjutor bishop from 1968 until O'Collins retired and handed him the episcopal ring.

Mulkearns was a tall, solidly built man with a head of thick, dark hair, greying at the sides. He walked with a rigid, precise gait. He was also an exacting man, aloof and authoritative, who spoke with a studied deliberation, as if his words carried more gravity than that of a mere mortal.

I've met other bishops, for whom a firm handshake was considered a perfectly acceptable greeting. Not Bishop Ronald Mulkearns. When I met him he deftly stuck his down-turned hand out at me. I'm not sure why but I puckered up and kissed his ring. There you go. A thousand old jokes revived in that one moment. But that was the way Mulkearns was—full of old Church conceit. Bow to me, boy!

While he was happy to demand a kiss on the episcopal ring from passers-by, he didn't lift a finger to stop Ridsdale and Day abusing children. The more I got to know him, the more I realised that it wasn't inertia or ineptitude. Like O'Collins, Mulkearns was just following orders. The Nuremburg Defence. If a priest was raping kids, it reflected poorly on the Church, all the way up to the Vatican. Move

Father John Michael Joseph Day as a
young priest in Horsham, circa 1945.
COURTESY BALLARAT DIOCESE

Denis Ryan as a police constable, fresh out of the academy. It would be four more years before he came across John Day in St Kilda.

Detective Denis Ryan not long after his arrival in Mildura.

Above: Jim Barritt (left) with his brothers, Barney (middle) and Denis (right).
NEWS LTD/NEWSPIX

Opposite above: Detective Denis Ryan (left) in Mildura in 1968 with police reservist Bill Brodie (right) and an unnamed colleague.

Opposite: Denis Ryan in Mildura in 2012.
SHARON LAPKIN

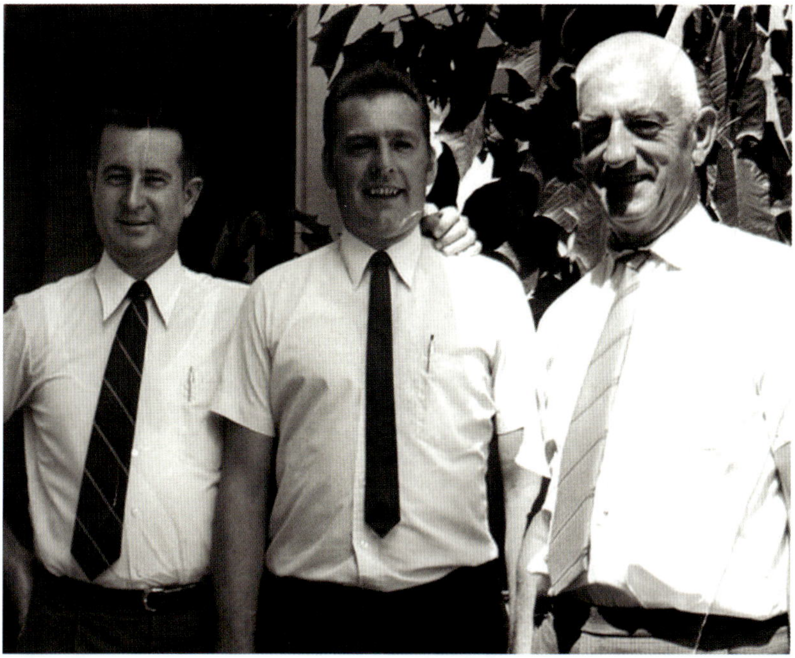

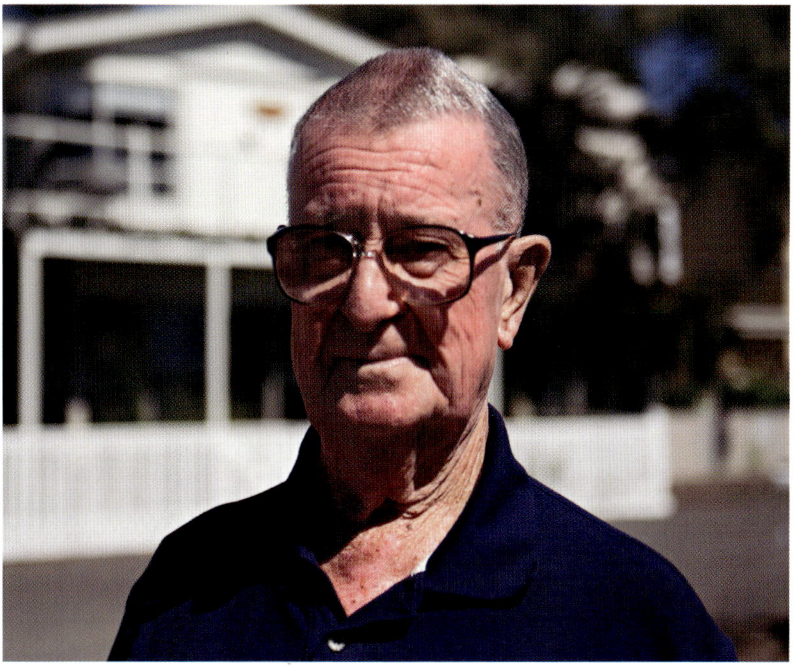

Gerald Ridsdale enters court in May 1993.
NEWS LTD/NEWSPIX/PETER WARD

Ridsdale, accompanied by George Pell,
back at court later that same year.
GEOFF AMPT/THE AGE

Denis Ryan at the grave of the paedophile priest, John Day. SHARON LAPKIN

Day's tombstone. 'Rest in Peace'. SHARON LAPKIN

Above: The Presbytery at Mildura where the Unholy Trinity planned their evil.

Opposite above: The church that Day built—the renovated Sacred Heart Peace Memorial Church, Mildura.

Opposite: Inside the vast church. The confession boxes are on the right.

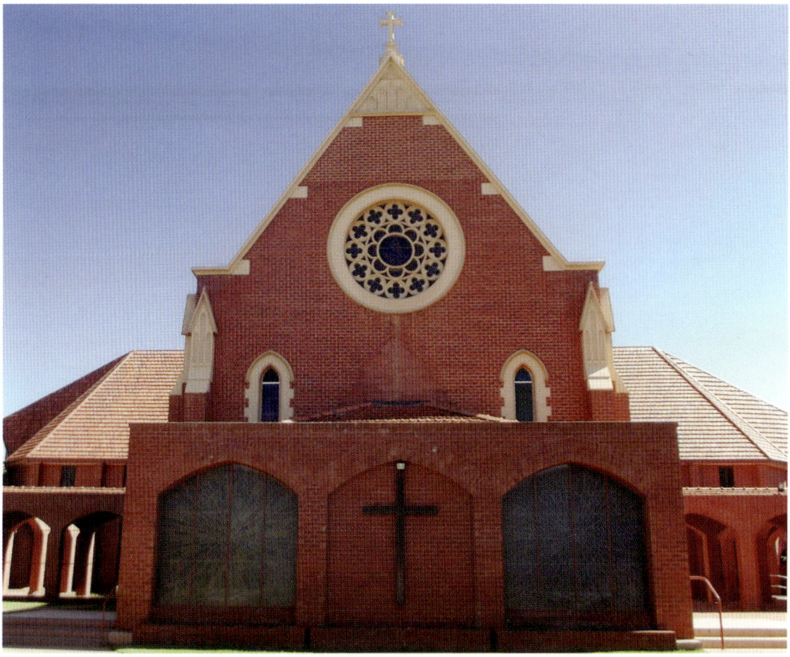

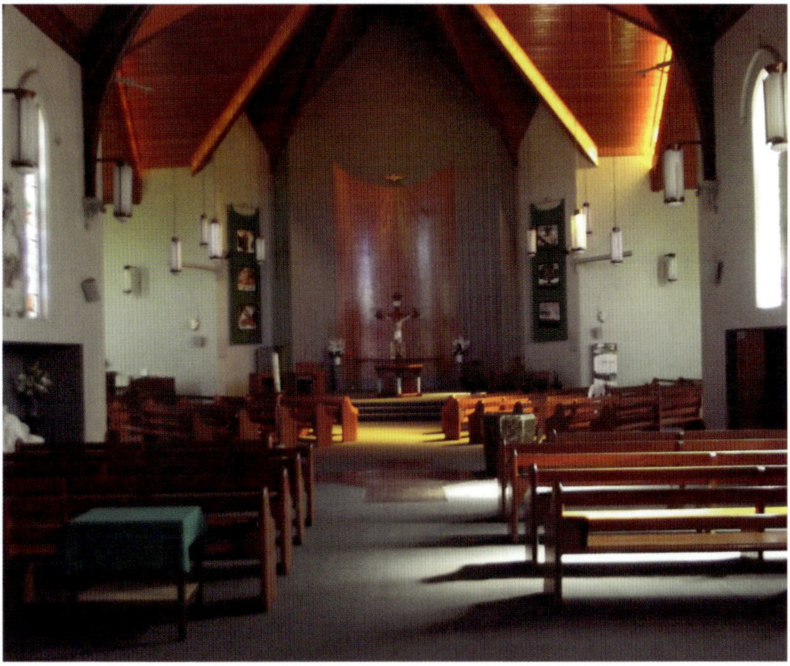

Top: Sacred Heart Primary School, Mildura.

Above: John Howden at his home in 2012.

Opposite: Religious warrior and made man in the Catholic Mafia, John 'Baton Jack' O'Connor guides author Frank Hardy into court in 1951. Hardy was facing charges of criminal defamation for his book, *Power Without Glory*. STAFF/THE AGE

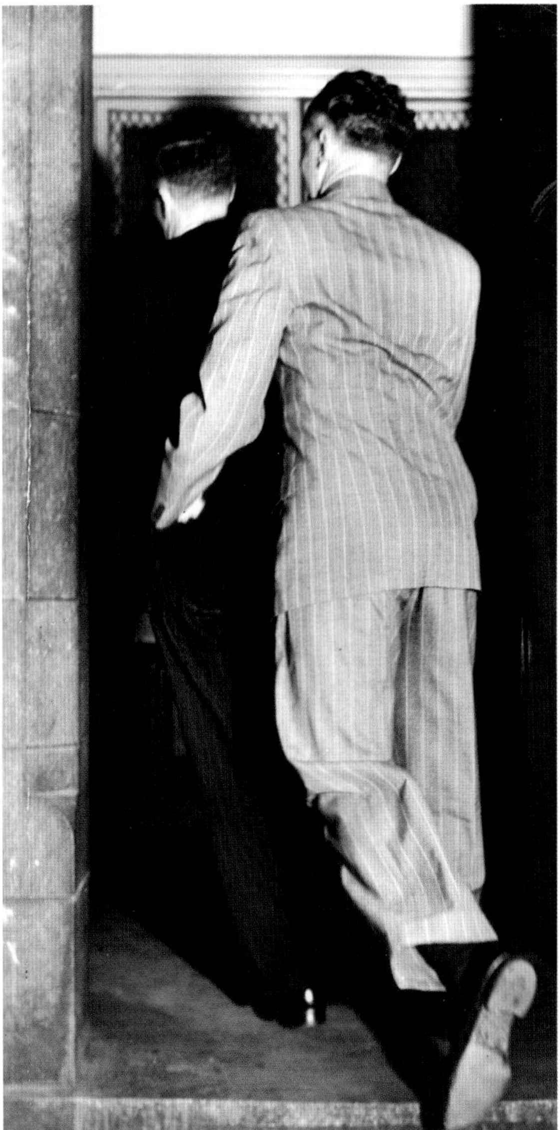

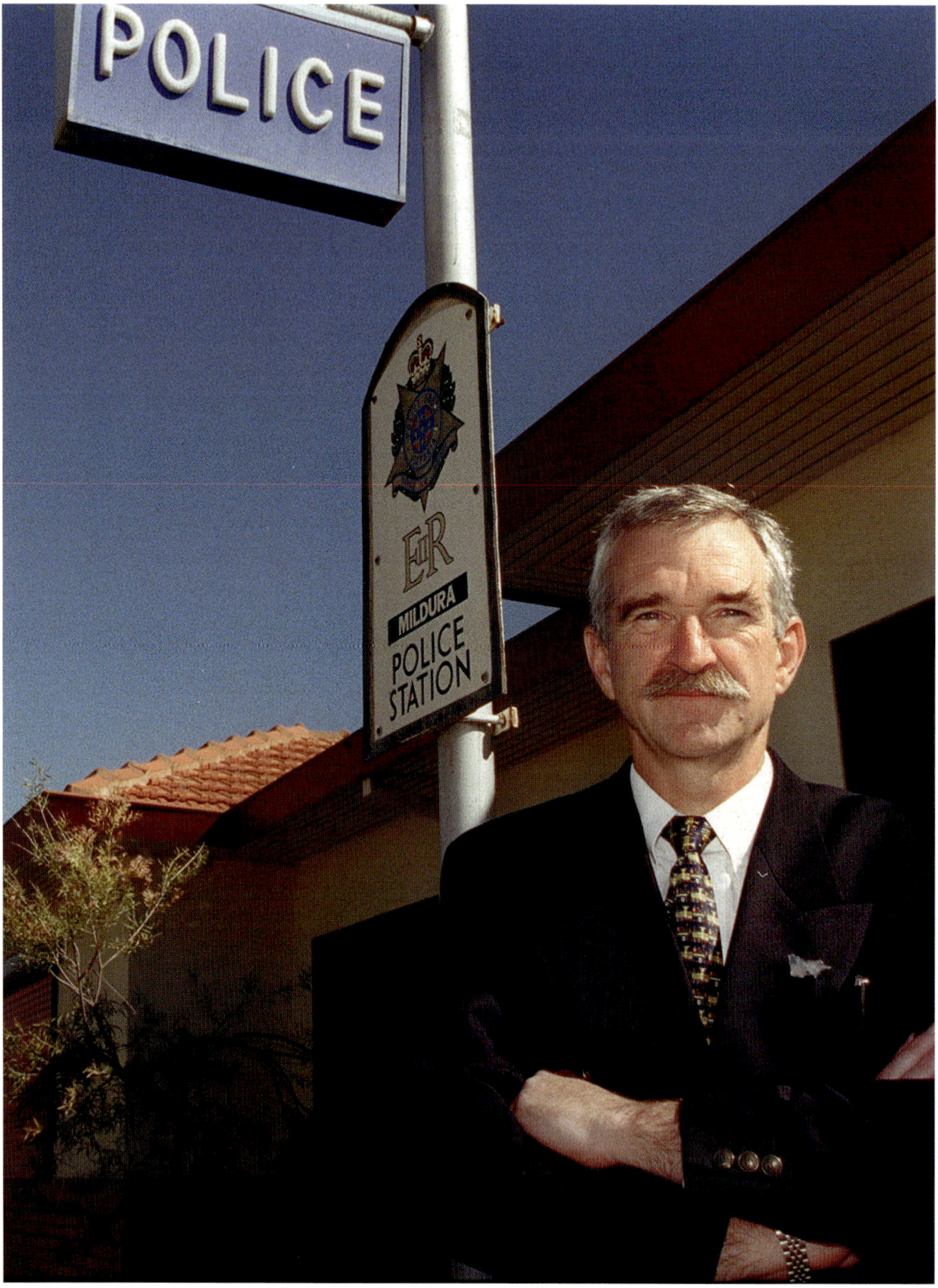

POLICE
EIIR
MILDURA
POLICE
STATION

Opposite: Independent Victorian MLA Russell Savage outside the Mildura Police Station. VINCE CALIGIURI/THE AGE

Above: Life goes on for John Fitzgibbon at his home in Mildura in 2012.

Standing tall. Kym Burford at Red Cliffs
in 2012.

the priest on and consign the victims to earthly oblivion.

If the police intervened, stare them down. If one copper could not be stared down, the Catholic Mafia within the police force would come to the rescue. It was a perfect situation. Flawless. And it had been going on for decades.

Until I came along and buggered up their cosy little conspiracy.

I'll be honest. If they had been drink-driving or shoplifting offences, if priests had broken into houses and knocked off TVs, I probably would have walked away, under pressure from the Church and the shadowy group within the police force that went all the way to the assistant commissioner. But priests were raping kids and I would not let that go.

❖

As the winter chill fell on Mildura in 1971, all I knew was that Day was a priest as well as a brothel-creeper and arrogant bastard who picked parishioners' pockets at Sunday mass and frequented prostitutes in Melbourne.

By this time my professional relationship with Barritt had become totally dysfunctional. I'd developed a manner of communicating with him that at least kept me sane. I'd never discuss real crime or any ongoing investigation with him. I'd stick to gossip, something he revelled in. If I heard of a bit of a fracas at a pub, I'd let him know. Usually, he was the one with the rumours.

'Ah, there's drunks comin' out of the Grand,' he'd say, with a gleam in his eye. It seemed that was all he was interested in talking to me about anyway.

Barritt held the world record in locking up drunks. He'd

wade in and clear a pub in twenty minutes, filling our lockup in one fell swoop, as if by osmosis. I'd seen him arrest men who hadn't touched a drop for public drunkenness.

❖

I was at my desk on a Wednesday morning. Barritt was out of the office up to God knows what. The previous Saturday my team, St Kilda, had been beaten by Hawthorn in the Aussie Rules grand final down in Melbourne. It was a roughhouse affair and people in Mildura were still talking about it. I copped a bit of ribbing around the station but I pretended not to care—I was a Rugby League follower and a St George man, really. What hurt more was that the Dragons had gone down 16–10 to their old foes, Souths, in the Sydney Rugby League grand final the weekend before.

The phone rang and I grabbed it.

'It's John Howden here, Denis.'

Howden was the senior master at St Joseph's College. I'd met him once at the Working Man's Club. He had a reputation for being a very fine teacher and an asset to the school. A strong, thickset bloke in his late thirties with wavy dark hair, he was a tough Aussie Rules footballer who'd won the medal in the local comp. Even then he was fit and strong, with a prominent jaw that underlined his strength.

'I need you to come up to the college,' Howden told me. 'There is a matter I wish to discuss.'

'All right. I can be up there within the hour.'

I was about to put the phone down when I heard Howden say, 'Don't let Jim Barritt know I've called. I'll explain when you get here.'

I told Bill Brodie I was heading out but gave no details about where I was going.

I knocked once on Howden's office door in the bowels of the school and the door swung open immediately. Howden was standing there with a tall, elderly nun. He introduced her to me as Sister Pancratius, a teaching principal at the school. The sister offered a firm, curt greeting, standing as straight as the flagpole in the schoolyard.

Howden and Pancratius looked at each other before Howden cleared his throat and spoke.

'The mother of one of our students has made a complaint that Monsignor John Day has indecently assaulted her daughter on a number of occasions.'

I was taken aback. I thought I knew Day's history as well as anyone. Prostitutes, yes. Did his depravity now extend to forcing himself upon schoolgirls?

Sister Pancratius waited for silence to fall before she spoke up.

'I have known about Monsignor Day's behaviour for some time now. It runs contrary to my vows of silence to say this to you, and I will never repeat what I have said from this moment forward,' she said. There was a sad resolve in her words. It was clear that she would consign her admission into the deep recesses of her mind and would never consider it again.

'I am pleased to meet you, Detective Ryan,' the sister said, and with that she walked past me and out of Howden's office, closing the door firmly behind her.

Howden then told me the girl's name and recounted her allegations. Day had touched her breasts while she was washing his car.

'I'll have to make a formal inquiry into these allegations,' I told him. 'I'll need to take statements from the girl and her mother. When can I see them?'

Howden made a call to the girl's mother. It was agreed that I would visit them at their home and conduct the interview there the following day.

'I wanted to speak to you. Not Barritt,' Howden told me. 'Barritt has a very close association with Monsignor Day. I fear the complaint would have gone nowhere.'

'What goes on here will not be shared with Barritt,' I said. 'I'll conduct the investigation myself and I'll keep in touch with you. This will stay between you and me until my inquiries have concluded.'

I thought, what the hell is going on here? My boss had a collection of child pornography in his desk. I had the circuit magistrate telling me that Barritt was obtaining statements from young women that were lurid to the point of obscenity I had Day's behaviour at St Kilda years before, and both Barritt's and Day's lies about Day at Apollo Bay.

The following day, I drove out to the girl's house. I could have taken a policewoman with me but I thought that would be unwise—it would place that officer under huge pressure. If one word of this got to Barritt, the investigation was over.

I met the mother first. She was a devout Catholic who had been involved in various groups and committees associated with Sacred Heart. She gave a statement that she signed in my presence, stating her daughter had informed her that she had been indecently assaulted by Day on a number of occasions.

The young girl, a boarder at the school for a number of years, then provided me with a statement alleging that Day had fondled her breast when he took her for a drive in his car. Another boarder was always present. The two girls would sit with Day on the front bench seat of his big car. He would put his arm around her while driving the car and touch her breast, tapping her nipple with his fingers to induce a sexual response. She said that this had occurred on five separate occasions. She had been 12 years of age when these offences occurred.

Both mother and daughter confirmed they had reported these incidents to Sister Euphemia, a nun and teacher at the school, shortly after they had occurred.

I wondered why the mother had not come to me at the time the offences occurred, and why she had sat on these allegations for so long. But it's easy to judge from a distance. Day was the tyrant; Barritt, the thug; and Kearney, the conman. The trinity was indestructible, seemingly immune to the challenges offered by a mother and daughter.

The mother understood that the Catholic Church would come down hard on them. Stories of shame and scandal would be circulated, false allegations made, and their lives opened up to a scrutiny that few could survive—a whispering campaign that would cast them adrift in this closed community. What hope did they have?

None.

As sexual assaults on minors go, what the mother and daughter had alleged was at the low end of the scale. I certainly don't mean to trivialise the offences Day committed against this young girl. She was hurt and damaged by the experience; she would be for many years.

The daughter also told me a story she had heard from one of her classmates. Day had insinuated himself on the girl on the drive home from Melbourne.

The following day I obtained a statement from this girl, who was in her leaving year at school at the time. She alleged that Day had indecently assaulted her when she was in grade six at Sacred Heart. She and four other girls had gone with Day and two nuns to see *The Sound of Music* in Melbourne. Day's car was packed—seven passengers in all, with him in the driver's seat. On the drive home, Day had asked the young girl to get in the front seat between him and the two nuns.

He told the 12-year-old girl to put her head in his lap while he drove. At various times on the long drive through the Mallee, he forced her head in to his groin, where she felt his erection beneath his trousers. It was night and the interior of the car was dark, but Day was so brazen as to do this in the presence of the two nuns—one of whom sat no more than half a metre away from him.

Sister Pancratius, the school principal who had withdrawn into silence, had implicitly acknowledged that there were more victims of Monsignor John Day in and around the school.

There was Day and the prostitutes. There were the photos in Barritt's desk drawer. There was Day, Barritt and Kearney meeting regularly at the presbytery, thick as thieves. The local yobbos, the louts of the town, all detested Day, yet they'd had almost nothing to do with him for years. And now two girls had come forward. I didn't have enough to charge Day with at that time; the statements from the girls were uncorroborated.

I needed to establish Day's pattern of behaviour. It was time to do a bit of digging into the monsignor.

There were a lot of unanswered questions. It was as if I was starting to piece a jigsaw together without knowing what the end result would look like, but with each piece the image before me grew darker and darker.

There was no point in going back to the school at this stage; that would only get back to Day. Then next thing I'd have Barritt on my back, and that would have been the end of it.

My next stop was to pay a visit to the local ne'er-do-wells, the young blokes in Mildura on whom Barritt and Day had continually waged war. These blokes, now in their twenties, had all attended Sacred Heart School. That would be a good start.

I saw Jimmy in Deakin Avenue, walking along the street on his way to the Wintersun Hotel. He walked with the swagger of a man who'd won his fair share of fist fights. We'd always got on all right. He saw me coming and grinned. He knew we were going to have one of our little chats.

'G'day, Mr Ryan. Beautiful day for it,' he said, his swagger becoming more exaggerated as he came nearer.

'G'day, Jimmy. Yeah. On your way to the Wintersun?'

'Nothin' wrong with that, Mr Ryan. A man's got to have a little fun.'

'Jimmy, I've got an inquiry going on. It's into your old mate, Monsignor Day.'

'About time you pulled up that dirty old bastard.'

'I need to tell you that anything you say to me is in the strictest confidence,' I said, looking him square in the eye.

'If this gets out, Day will find out about it and knock this over.'

Jimmy was silent for a while, his bravado slipping for just a moment.

'If I give you a name, would he get into any strife?'

'No. I would make sure he was looked after. Why, what do you know?'

'Well, the dirty bastard made him play with his old fella.'

'Who?'

He gave me the name of a bloke, a plumber called Kym Burford. I'd never heard of him but he'd been at Sacred Heart before going on to St Joseph's.

'Is he the only one you know of?' I asked.

'Yep. That's it.' Jimmy was pretty keen to get on his way.

'All right. Good on you, Jimmy. You have a good day.'

I rang Kym at his home. His wife answered and told me he was at the Working Man's Club. I rang him there and told him I needed him to come in to see me.

'I haven't done anything wrong,' he told me.

'No, you're not in any trouble, mate. I just need your help.'

I had to make a time that would suit Kym but also a time when I knew Barritt was unlikely to be in the office. That wasn't easy, as Barritt came and went as he chose. Evenings were best. Kym agreed to see me almost straight away. It had just gone six o'clock.

Just in case, I kept my office door closed in an effort to stop the stupid big bastard from sticking his head in.

At the time, Kym Burford was 26 years of age, married, with a couple of young children. He was doing pretty well for himself. He was rough around the edges, but as I got to know him better, he came across as a very decent fellow.

He was still toey, worried I might have him in the frame over some business or other. I tried to put him at ease as quickly as I could.

'I'm conducting an inquiry into the behaviour of Monsignor Day, but it is a very discrete investigation because of the close relationship between Day and Detective Sergeant Barritt, which you probably know well.'

'Yes, I do,' Kym said.

'I've been told that Day indecently dealt with you when you were an altar boy. You must realise that this must stop. It's ruining the lives of people left, right and centre. With your co-operation, we can prevent Day from continuing to abuse young children in the future.'

He nodded. 'Yeah, all right. I hate that bastard Day. I gave the Catholic Church away completely after that. Never set foot in a bloody church since.'

'What did Day do to you?'

'He tried to root me.'

'How old were you when this happened?'

'I was at Sacred Heart in grade six. I would have been 11.'

Kym provided a statement detailing one episode in 1957, when he had travelled with Day and his housekeeper, Sarah Lane, in Day's car, then a Ford Fairlane, to Melbourne via Ararat. The housekeeper got out at Ararat to visit relatives.

For the remainder of the trip to Melbourne, Day sat with his penis exposed, periodically grabbing the boy's hand and demanding that he play with it. Kym tried to resist but the small, thin 11-year-old boy was overpowered by Day.

That evening Day and Kym went to Day's sister's house in Williamstown. There was only one bed for them to sleep in and, in the course of the night, Kym had woken to Day attempting to force his erect penis into his anus. Kym resisted, and Day stopped. The following day, after a trip to a cinema in Melbourne and during the return journey to Mildura, Day committed several more sexual assaults on the young boy.

It transpired that Kym had been on at least five trips to Melbourne with Day in his car, and on these occasions the priest committed numerous sexual assaults and acts of gross indecency on the 11-year-old. Kym said he hated these trips, and whenever Day invited him he always declined. However, as he was in the care of two aunts—both Catholic zealots who worshipped Day—the priest would invariably approach the two women, who gave their consent.

Day had carefully selected his young victim. The boy was unable to resist physically and his aunts' devotion to the Church ensured he was unable to avoid Day's perverted acts.

Kym Burford then signed his statement.

Had I been naive? Had my own faith blinded me to the obvious? Could I have pulled Day up earlier and protected at least some of his victims from harm? These thoughts weigh heavily on me to this day.

The notion of paedophile priests in the Catholic Church is now deeply embedded in the public's consciousness, but in 1971 the thought of such a thing was anathema. No priests had been brought before the courts. Entrenched paedophilia in the Church was a dirty secret, kept by the perpetrators and their victims, then covered up by the Church and a handful of police who actively thwarted any serious investigation on the rare occasions that complaints were made.

Over the next couple of weeks I took statements from more of Day's victims. There was a certain ease to the investigation. Each victim gave me another name, and that person would give me another. Kym had been assaulted and raped in 1957. Another victim, a boy of 15, had been sexually assaulted by Day in 1970.

Thirteen years. Five confirmed victims. Numerous counts of indecent assault, gross indecency and buggery.

The information flowed from the victims in their statements and records of interview. Other victims, other leads for me to pursue, were mentioned. This told me that Day had many more victims. Perhaps hundreds.

I had great difficulty comprehending it. Priests, even a brothel-creeper like Day, were held in high regard. They held positions of trust in the community. They were the spiritual guardians of their parishioners—men, women and children.

Despite the encounter in St Kilda years before, it was beyond my understanding that Day would force himself on children as young as 8 years of age. It was the last thing I would ever have expected, and I was a seasoned detective who'd seen his fair share of the dark side of the human spirit. It was a jolt to my system. I felt disgusted, sickened to the core. I really wanted to punch the living shit out of Day and give him a stomping for good measure. It might have felt good for a moment but it would have been the end for me had I fronted him with fists and feet. It would have been the end of the investigation, too.

I kept dwelling on what John Howden had told me: 'Avoid Barritt at all costs.'

My senior officer. My boss. I always thought he was as useless as pockets on a singlet but keeping him out of the picture—due to his friendship with Day—had a darker subtext. It was a rolled gold certainty that Barritt would have stymied my investigation. Howden understood it. I knew it, too. The question was, why would he?

It's not unheard of for a copper to go into bat for a mate—pull a few strings, make a blue disappear. But there was more to this than mateship, and Day's crimes were far from trivial. Worse than murder in my view. Young lives viciously assaulted. Trust destroyed. Futures stolen.

My boss was Day's protector. What did Barritt know of Day's perversions? What did Joe Kearney know? They'd have to have been a couple of blind Freddies, and deaf and dumb as well, not to know.

The senior uniform officer at Mildura was Inspector Alby Irwin. When he first came to Mildura we got on well. I'd had him over to my place for barbecues on a few occasions. We got drunk and sang songs. Both he and his wife could drink for Australia. He had been a pretty good bloke and a supporter of mine.

Irwin was a thickset fellow with an enormous stomach that hung over the belt of his strides. Most of us put his oversize belly down to his love of the drink. It turned out that his gargantuan gut was the result of an enormous but benign tumour, which was surgically removed in the winter of 1971.

Something strange must have happened to Alby when he was under anaesthesia. After his recovery, his waistband went down eight sizes but his capacity for religious fervour increased exponentially. He started to see God in the trees. He was the first person at mass on Sundays and even swore off the grog. More troubling was the fact that he had become very close to Barritt and, through him, was drawn into the orbit of Day.

I had one mate I could rely on and trust—Harry Herbert, a fellow detective in the CIB. I could share my thoughts with him over a few beers. He was a strange fish in the force, neither a Catholic nor a Freemason. Harry was great company, a bit of a knockabout like me. He'd played football for Geelong and was a hell of a cricketer, a fast bowler who once ripped through the English in a tour match. England captain Sir Leonard Hutton described Harry as the fastest bowler he'd ever faced.

I'd told Harry about the statements I had from the two girls. I reckoned it was the tip of a much bigger and uglier iceberg. Harry agreed.

But Harry pulled out. He sought a transfer back to Melbourne, and he got it.

'I'm leaving you, Din,' Harry said. Just like that. I couldn't believe what I was hearing. Harry babbled something about how he and his wife had to get back to Melbourne. The tenants in his house in Melbourne had smashed the place up.

Years later, after Harry's death, his wife Lynette told me she had wanted him out of Mildura. She knew about Day; Harry had told her. She knew the shit was going to hit the fan and she didn't want her husband around when it happened.

As a detective, I was on my own. How the hell was I going to handle this without any support?

I was a month into the investigation when I made up my mind to approach the most senior officer in the district—Superintendent Jack McPartland, who was based at Swan Hill.

Jack was a devout Catholic, but he was 222 kilometres and a virtual world away from the cloying atmosphere in Mildura driven by Barritt, Day and Kearney. I expected Jack to offer his support and guide me through the investigation. I rang him up and told him where my inquiry into Day had taken me.

'I've got five statements from victims alleging that Monsignor Day has committed numerous acts of sexual assault, gross indecency and attempted buggery,' I said.

I expected a pause, a moment of silence while Jack reflected on the best way to proceed, but he fired back without hesitation.

'I want you to give these statements to Inspector Irwin straight away and to cease any further inquiries,' he said. 'You are no longer involved in this investigation.'

I couldn't believe what I was hearing. Jack wanted me to deliver the evidence I had obtained against Day directly into the belly of the beast.

McPartland was my senior officer but I felt I had to challenge him.

'One moment, sir,' I said in my most polite voice. 'You're asking me to deliver these statements to Inspector Irwin, a man who is a bosom friend of Jim Barritt. And Barritt is in turn the best friend of Monsignor Day. That will be the end of this inquiry.'

'I have given you an instruction,' he replied. 'I expect you to obey it.'

'But . . . but . . . What you're asking me to do will effectively destroy this investigation,' I blurted out.

'I'm going to tell you something now, Detective Ryan, and you're not going to like it. I'm a Superintendent and you're a nobody. Do as you're fucking told.'

McPartland slammed the phone down in my ear.

I sat at my desk, bewildered. I was so angry I could barely think. I took some deep breaths and let my fury subside.

I remembered the voice of Fred Russell, the detective sergeant who had fronted me at O'Connor's in Spencer Street over a decade before, asking me if I wanted to join an exclusive group of Catholic detectives who took their orders directly from the Cathedral. I thought it was traffic offences. The odd drink-drive. A drunken priest picking up prostitutes. Surely this group would not sink so low as to pull up an investigation into a priest raping kids?

The Catholic Mafia, active and influential in Melbourne, had spread its tentacles into Mildura, where it was protecting this paedophile priest.

I did as I was told—well, overtly at least. I handed over the five statements I had obtained to Alby Irwin. I could tell Irwin had been given a heads-up. He took the statements without a word, then he just looked up at me for a moment before returning to his paperwork.

It was obvious that this inquiry was headed for the dust bin. How can human beings—let alone policemen—fail the people, the children, they had sworn to protect so utterly?

I had followed orders, but by the time I left Irwin's office I'd made another decision. I wasn't going to drop this, no matter who gave the order. They could all go and get fucked.

7

THE SMOTHER

The truth is incontrovertible, malice may attack it, ignorance may deride it, but in the end; there it is.
WINSTON CHURCHILL, 1874–1965

By the end of January 1972, I had interviewed twelve of Monsignor Day's victims. They all provided statements, alleging the priest had raped and indecently assaulted them. The Mildura allegations ran across thirteen years. I hadn't touched on Day's time at Colac, Apollo Bay, Beech Forest, Horsham or Ararat. The twelve victims I'd found—altar boys, gymnasts and boys and girls at Sacred Heart Primary School and St Joseph's College—had all been children in Mildura.

I could have found a hundred victims in Mildura, maybe more. Day had been at Colac for three years, Apollo Bay for three, Beech Forest for two, Horsham for two, Ararat for nine. He was a younger man then. God only knows what carnage he had perpetrated in these places.

How many victims were there? How many policemen had been directed not to continue an investigation into Day over that time? How many had had their concerns assuaged by Day's facilitator, Bishop O'Collins?

Officially, I was off the case. Barritt had ordered me onto divisional duties with the uniform boys—the police equivalent of being sent to Coventry. I came into the office one day and found a report from Barritt on my desk. I was going to be working 3 pm to 11 pm. It was just Barritt trying to get me out of the way, keeping me busy on the sort of work I'd done after I'd left the academy. That was that. I was out on the road each day. He didn't say a word. We were no longer on speaking terms.

❖

Irwin had interviewed Day back on 10 November 1971. He took Barritt with him, just to make sure it was a complete balls up. I suppose Irwin thought he was doing me a courtesy when he told me he and Barritt were on their way to interview Day at the presbytery. Irwin handed me a blank record of interview with the questions he was going to ask Day already typed in. I exploded.

'You're taking Barritt with you? He's Day's best friend! This is contrary to everything you were taught as a detective. You are totally and completely compromising the investigation. Your record of interview is a disgrace. I'd expect better from a first year constable fresh out of the academy.'

Irwin leapt about a metre into the air.

'What are you talking about? How dare you say that to me?'

His voice was shaking with anger and he got into a fighting stance.

I did the same and waited for him to throw the first punch. He looked at me, then thought better of engaging in a stoush. He turned his back on me and walked away.

Barritt had a copy of the record of interview and that meant Day had a copy, too. He would not only know the questions he was going to be asked but also who had made the allegations against him. It was a farce, a perversion. Gross negligence explained it to a point. But this was worse. This was wilful.

Years later, I obtained a copy of the completed record of interview. Day denied everything, as I had expected. But there is a coolness and a certainty to his answers that told me he anticipated every question during that interview.

Day was not issued with a caution at any time. Irwin virtually apologised for the inconvenience of asking Day questions about him raping kids.

'As you know Monsignor, Irwin is my name, Inspector of Police, and my colleague is Senior Detective Barritt. I am making inquiries into allegations that have been levelled at you concerning acts of attempted buggery, gross indecency and indecent assaults committed on young people, boys and girls over a period of thirteen years from 1957. I intend asking you questions which I have prepared and I also intend recording your answers. Have you any objection to this procedure?'

Of course Day had no objections. The interview was a charade. And Day's best mate, Jim Barritt—the scourge of Mildura—sat across the table.

Just three Catholics sitting in a room having a chat.

After Irwin interviewed Day I handed him statements from two further victims, young boys who both alleged Day had indecently assaulted them and subjected them to acts of gross indecency while they were at St Joseph's. Irwin snatched them out of my hand like I'd handed him yesterday's sandwiches.

When I was in the police force down in Melbourne, I'd come across my fair share of standover men. If anyone had told me then that I'd be threatened by a Catholic priest, I would have fallen over laughing, but that's what happened in Mildura after I started investigating Day.

In early December 1971 I was in the watch house having a chat with some of the uniform boys. Laurie McGrath, a senior constable, came in and told me that someone who wanted to talk to me was in his car outside.

'Who is it, Laurie?'

Either Laurie didn't hear me or he pretended not to, so I made my way outside. There was Father Peter Taffe, sitting in his car, right out the front. I'd known Taffe around Sacred Heart. He'd been a priest at Mildura for three years or so, and on one occasion I'd had a beer with him at the Working Man's Club.

'Did you want to see me, Peter?'

He leant over the passenger seat.

'Drop the inquiry into Monsignor Day or you'll be out of a job.'

My hackles rose at a hundred miles an hour.

'You can go and get fucked, pal.'

He glared back at me briefly then gunned the motor and drove off.

He was prophetic, I'll give Father Taffe that, but when did the Roman Catholic Church start running protection rackets, and why did Father Taffe think the Church had some say over the hire and fire authority within the Victoria Police force?

❖

Mildura was abuzz with rumour and gossip. The Catholics were divided almost straight down the line. One half supported me, the other half would have been happy to see me burnt at the stake as a heretic. The non-Catholics in Mildura thought it reaffirmed their faith to see the parish priest, the recently anointed Monsignor Day, and his copper mate, Jim Barritt, face scandal and innuendo.

It got to the point where I couldn't walk down the street without someone making a passing comment to me—some were vindictive and vitriolic, others supportive and sympathetic.

On one occasion I was walking down Langtree Avenue, along the strip of shops and past the chemist shop, Israel and Deacon. Frank Deacon, the local chemist, charged out of his store and fronted me.

'I've a good mind to give you a bloody thumping, Ryan,' he said, trying to look his most menacing. 'Bringing disgrace on our Church.'

He was my age. He was my height. He had a few more kilos on him than I did but I wasn't overly troubled.

'Grow up, Frank. I've had a hard enough time of it without you adding to the insanity,' I said, trying to get past him.

'I'm serious, Ryan. I'll drop you.'

I burst out laughing. I couldn't help it. There was me in a desperate struggle with Barritt, Irwin and McPartland, not to mention Day, and now I was being fronted by the local chemist, looking for a blue. But my amusement only enraged him further. I knew he wasn't a brawler, but he stuck his chest out a bit further just to show he was not going to back down. The next step was the tricky part for Frank. It was either throw a punch or back off. I gave him the choice.

'You just bloody watch yourself, Ryan. That's all I'm saying.' And he made a strategic retreat back to his pharmacy.

Thirteen days after Irwin and Barritt interviewed Day, Irwin prepared a report to Superintendent McPartland that effectively killed off the investigation. I didn't know it at the time. No one told me. Irwin had smothered the case.

I came across his report years later. It cited a bizarre example of a case of bestiality, allegedly committed in 1842 but not complained about until 1844, as a reason for not proceeding against Day. The judge had determined that the case should not proceed, given the length of time between the alleged offence and the time the complaint had been heard. How this was relevant to the by then seven complainants being indecently assaulted and raped by a priest is anybody's guess.

Irwin concluded his report with the words: 'It is my recommendation that no further police action be taken in this matter.'

A week later, McPartland followed suit, forwarding Irwin's report to Reg Jackson, the Chief Commissioner, with a couple of his own remarks thrown in for good measure. McPartland agreed with Irwin that: 'The persons who have made these allegations, so many years after the alleged incidents, may be regarded as accomplices, in need of corroboration.' Bad enough to be raped by a priest: Jack McPartland thought the victims may have committed crimes in cahoots with Day.

His report was a carbon copy of Irwin's and the recommendations were the same. Kill the investigation. No further inquiries. No new evidence to be considered. Move along. Nothing to see here.

But there *was* new evidence. On 8 December I interviewed a boy, a student at St Joseph's, who alleged that Monsignor Day had indecently assaulted him in December 1970, when he had spent a night with Day in a motel room. Another boy was present but that boy's father would not allow me to interview him.

There were now three signed statements from current students at St Joseph's College. I had to tell John Howden. I'd not spoken to him at all since he had alerted me to the first allegation against Day. I met him at the school and told him that eight victims of Day's paedophilia had now come forward. All had attended St Joseph's College.

I also told him that Superintendent McPartland had ordered me off the case. But there was more bad news: with me off the case, Irwin had taken charge and Barritt had insinuated himself into the investigation. I told him that Day had been interviewed and while I hadn't seen Day's response, it was clear the interview had been a farrago.

Howden was appalled. This had now become a serious duty of care issue for the senior master. But Howden had a bomb of his own to drop. A couple of weeks earlier, a nun and principal at Sacred Heart Primary School had come to him with a complaint. She had discovered that Joe Kearney was cooking the books: the government had been paying the salary of a teacher who didn't exist. Day had signed off on all the accounts. The sister at Sacred Heart knew that Day was aware of the phantom teacher, too.

Howden had raised the matter at a meeting of parishioners at the parish hall. Day had dismissed the accusations out of hand but it was impossible to walk away from the obvious fact that the Commonwealth was paying the salary of a teacher who did not exist into the school's accounts. Day could play a straight bat to the parish at large, where he still had many supporters.

Howden and a group of other senior parishioners decided to confront Day at the presbytery about the fraud, and try to determine where the money had gone. According to Howden, Day was at his ugliest at this meeting. He continued to deny and obfuscate, but Howden would not be placated. Day was backed into a corner.

'I'll see you in prison, Howden,' Day snarled as the meeting concluded.

No one ever did find out where the money had gone. No doubt some had found its way into the building fund and other accounts related to the parish, but a lot of the money must have simply ended up in the pockets of Day and Kearney. Howden told me that some of the parishioners were furious about the state of the parish's accounts and one, or perhaps more, might have already taken the matter to the police.

I knew nothing about it. If a complaint had been made, it had not come to me, which meant it was almost certainly in Barritt's hands.

There's no doubt it was a serious matter, but in my mind it was trivial compared to Day's crimes against children. The fraud was symptomatic of a wider problem—Day's treatment of the parish and its people as goods and chattels for him to use, abuse and pervert without let or hindrance.

The more momentous business at hand was to bring his sexual abuse to a halt.

It was my suggestion that we write to the Bishop of Ballarat. Howden agreed. We presumed that a Catholic bishop would hold to moral and lawful principles, that he would regard these allegations with the utmost seriousness and provide some sort of protection to Mildura's most vulnerable parishioners. We were naive.

That evening Howden and I hammered out a letter on one of the school's old typewriters. We agreed that Mulkearns had to be given as much information as possible, so we listed the names and the addresses of the victims, spelt out the nature of the allegations in detail and stated where the offences had occurred.

We sought some action from the bishop. Perhaps a meeting with a delegation of the parish could be arranged. First and foremost we sought Day's immediate removal from the parish. We both signed the letter and put it in the mail.

It was a last resort. Even at this time, I had no idea of the extent of the forces acting against me and the lengths to which the Church would go to ensure that Day's victims would never have the satisfaction of seeing him brought before the courts.

Anyway, it was done. Bishop Mulkearns would now be aware of the allegations. Under Church or canon law, he had the power to act against Day. He had the power to remove Day from Mildura and, as a moral arbiter, he had the responsibility to act and assist police with their inquiries.

I was being ingenuous. I am happy to admit that now, but the letter that Howden and I wrote was a simple and sincere attempt to get the bishop to intercede.

It only took a week for me to discover how wrong I had been. Both Howden and I received a written response from Mulkearns. The audacity of it was breathtaking. Ronald Mulkearns—Bishop of Ballarat, a man who had been a senior cleric in the diocese for three or more years—wrote a strident defence of Day. He had been made aware that Day had been cleared by Irwin, Barritt and, later, McPartland. That was good enough for him.

He failed to address the allegations made by the additional victims, and neither Barritt nor Irwin had raised these allegations in their interview with Day.

Mulkearns mentioned that he had received a complaint 'that Monsignor Day was misappropriating Parish funds' but did not indicate what action he was taking, or if he even intended taking any.

In regard to the sexual assaults, he relied on the findings of corrupt police. Barritt and Irwin had cleared Day, and now it was time for me to change my ways in a 'demonstration of loyalty to [Day] at a time he has been subjected to very great embarrassment and strain'.

I bristled as I read the letter. I was being told by a bishop that Irwin and Barritt had jumped on my investigation. My colleagues hadn't said a word to me. Not a peep. Yet the lines of communication between Irwin, Barritt and Mulkearns were clearly open. There was active collusion between Irwin, Barritt and the Church.

A week or so earlier, I was walking down past the courthouse when I saw Barritt and Kearney in the solicitor's room, flipping through the statements I had given to Irwin. I could see them muttering away, their brows furrowed, thinking up some new scheme to clear Day. They were in heavy self-preservation mode. If Day went, they were gone, too.

They saw me, a little too late, and turned around.

As I had suspected, Kearney was the conduit between Barritt and Mulkearns. He and Day had driven down to see Mulkearns in Ballarat to respond to the charges outlined in the letter Howden and I had written. Kearney had taken Irwin's confidential report, hot off the presses from Barritt. The report was not only confidential, it was also still winding its way to the chief commissioner's office for consideration.

Kearney and Day presented the bishop with the report that had summarily cleared Day. They put it all down to Howden hating Day and me despising Barritt. Nothing more than malicious gossip, My Lord. Like a hungry snapper, Mulkearns swallowed the nonsense whole.

While I remained unaware of Jack McPartland putting his 'Thus far and no further' stamp on Irwin's report, he had included with the usual caveat: 'I recommend that in all the circumstances, the brief be considered by a competent legal authority to determine what action, if any, would be taken.'

That meant it wasn't over and Day had not been cleared, although it was obvious that Irwin and Barritt had washed their hands of the investigation and would not pursue it further. That seemed to be the way more senior police up the line would call it, too.

It wasn't over as far as I was concerned. If Mulkearns, Irwin, Barritt and McPartland thought this investigation was done and dusted, I had news for them.

Not long after I had written the letter to Mulkearns, I received a call from an old mate in the social welfare office. Joe Kearney was in the frame for raping a single mother. My mate told me the woman had fled, having fought Kearney off and charged down onto Deakin Avenue, semi-naked, her blouse ripped open. She was hysterical and made her way across the road to the welfare office, where my mate and a female member of staff comforted her.

My mate, John Noble, and the female staff member had both encouraged the woman to go to the police and report the incident, but she refused to. As Kearney oversaw her child maintenance payments and required her to visit his office in order to receive them, she was too frightened to make a complaint.

I made some discreet inquiries with witnesses, who confirmed my mate's account of the incident, but Kearney's victim continued to refuse to make a complaint, so there was nothing I could do.

In the two weeks before Christmas 1971, I obtained three further statements from past students at Sacred Heart Primary School, all alleging they had been indecently assaulted by Day when they were aged between 11 and 13.

I was an experienced investigator but what struck me was the ease with which I could identify Day's victims and also, for the most part, their willingness to come forward. By

Christmas that year, I had eleven victims. I was convinced I could find many more.

It has to be remembered that at that time no priest had been convicted of child sex offences in Victoria or even in Australia, as far as I can tell. That wouldn't happen until 1978.

I didn't think to ask why no Catholic priest had ever found himself standing before a judge. Paedophile priests were not recognised at the time. The word 'paedophilia' was not known to me, nor was it in common use; it remained locked away in the obscurity of psychiatric jargon. Although the academics didn't know it and it was not discussed in any public forum, Australia was experiencing an epidemic of paedophilia. The centre of the epidemic was the Ballarat diocese, and many of the crimes were attributable to Catholic priests like Day and Ridsdale, who were at the absolute nadir of depravity, leaving literally thousands of victims in their wake.

What I did know was that I had a raving child sex offender who happened to be a monsignor in the Roman Catholic Church, and no one in the Church or the police force seemed to give two hoots about it. To me, on the scale of criminality, child sex offences were at least as serious as murder, perhaps even worse: their victims suffer pain and trauma and breaches of trust, and their lives are often dispatched to oblivion.

❖

I was alone and sailing in uncharted territory against the express orders of the police force I served. I needed someone to share this with. There was no one in the office I could open up to. Barritt looked at me like I was the shit on his shoes. Bill Brodie, the police reservist, had brushed me off; he'd barely said a word to me since the investigation began.

Harry Herbert's replacement at the CIB was Graham McAllister, who had come up from Melbourne. On his second day in Mildura, I asked him if he wanted to join me for a drink at the Working Man's Club. I knew he wasn't the sort of bloke who'd say no to a beer. But he knocked me back all the same.

'I've been told by senior officers in Melbourne not to discuss anything with you,' he said. 'Keep out of my way.'

Nice to meet you, too, Graham.

Jean bore the brunt of it. The CIB motto was 'Never take your work home with you', and I'd stuck by that religiously. I had established a divide between my work as a police officer and my life as a husband and father. But this was different. It was simply too big to keep under my hat. I told Jean what Day had been up to but I deliberately left out the specifics of the case. It would be too traumatic for her, and it was also part of what I considered to be an ongoing investigation. She knew of my antipathy towards Barritt, going back to my first day on duty in Mildura. I told her that Barritt was trying to shoot me down and that he was protecting this monster. Every senior copper in the district was lining up to do the same.

It was a heavy burden to place on her. Perhaps I was selfish. There were things in Jean's background that made Day's sexual assaults and breaches of trust very difficult for her to process emotionally. She had never known who her father was. She couldn't remember her mother. When she was an infant during the Depression, Jean had been offered in a newspaper advertisement. A husband and wife had taken her on, and she grew up in their family, never formally adopted, made to feel like a square peg in a round hole from day one.

Just after we were married, Jean told me she had been sexually molested from the age of 9 until she was about 14 by her guardian and father figure. She had hated this man's obscene attentions. The husband and wife were devoted Methodists at the time. Afterwards I learnt they had joined the Salvation Army, and that this child molester used to bang the drum in one of their bands.

When Jean had converted to Catholicism seven years earlier, she did so out of love for me and the boys, but she had been betrayed before by people who were overtly religious, purportedly living in a God-fearing household while behaving in a less than spiritual fashion behind closed doors.

She urged me on with the investigation. She was disgusted with the overall picture I painted of Day and his perverse attentions to children. I had no idea at the time just how deeply this investigation would affect her.

Jean and I talked about the boys. Michael was in year eight at St Joseph's College. Martin, Gavin and Anthony were at St Joseph's Primary School in Red Cliffs, far enough away from the clutches of Day. Michael and Martin had both heard the rumours about Day, which by then were swirling around St Joseph's.

After I made a delicate but firm inquiry, Michael told Jean and me that he hadn't had any trouble with Day. I wanted all the boys to continue with a Catholic education at St Joseph's in Mildura. The shadow of Day hung over the school but I knew that, while good people like Howden were in control and Day's crimes were coming to light, the boys were safe.

At no time did my investigation of Day interfere with my faith, but the moral corruption of the Church and its complete disregard for the laws of the land in relation to the conduct of its priests was becoming obvious. But I stuck by my faith. Some people may think this odd and will wonder why I didn't walk away from the Roman Catholic Church. My faith was unshakable. I will remain a Roman Catholic to the day I die. I wasn't going to let bastards like Day, Mulkearns and O'Connor destroy my faith.

I wasn't going to let them bugger up my Christmas either.

The Christmas break is a great down time around Australia. It's not so for coppers. Every year I would try to take the main public holidays off, but would have to work the rest. I was on call all the time.

Christmas at the Ryan household was a family affair. We'd go to mass at Red Cliffs in the morning. Jean would be in the kitchen cooking the turkey while the boys and I would be out the back playing cricket. The boys and I would set the table, which would heave with food, and then the feasting would begin.

I was determined that this Christmas would be the same happy time it had always been for the Ryan family at Red Cliffs. Like any good copper, I thought I could compartmentalise my investigation into Day. Outwardly, I guess, I was successful. Certainly I tried to give Jean and the kids no clue. I'd been able to do it with gruesome murders. I'd pulled decomposing bodies out of houses and seen them fall apart in my hands. I'd photographed crime scenes where people had been blown apart with shotgun blasts. I thought I had seen the worst that humanity could throw up but I'd always finish my shift, go home and sleep well, sometimes with a few grogs under my belt to help erase the memory. Counselling for police in those days came in the form of drinking thirty beers in the pub, going home drunk, waking up with a hangover. Drinking to forget.

But I couldn't forget the situation in Mildura, nor did I try to erase the shock and disgust at the front of my mind.

For the first time in my life, I started experiencing nightmares about Day, though I hadn't seen him for months. There were two recurring dreams. The first had me looking at a little boy, 8 to 10 years of age, with his pants pulled down, forced over a bed. The kid was weeping while Day, dressed in his priestly garments, straddled him and sodomised him. In the other, I would see Day standing in his black shirt, dog collar and black pants while a young boy knelt in front of him, playing with his exposed penis. This boy was wailing in pain and torment, too. I'd wake with a start each time, in a cold, clammy sweat. The nightmare visions were vivid representations of reality. Day had done these things. I was the only police officer in Mildura who gave a damn. The others—Barritt, Irwin and McPartland—were protecting him so he could continue to rape children.

To this day I continue to see the mongrel in my nightmares. I saw him in the flesh just once more at Red Cliffs Church. This church was a haven. In my six years attending mass at the church, I'd never seen him there.

Jean, Michael, Gavin and Anthony were sitting with me in the pews. We saw Martin, who was one of the altar boys, pass by in his red smock as the procession made its way to the altar. The Red Cliffs priest, Father Anthony Del Bollo, was next, and behind him was Day in his full monsignor's regalia, looking pompous and arrogant. As the congregation started to sit, I grabbed Jean's attention.

'Jean, you take the three boys to the side door and wait for me.'

She nodded, and started to lead Michael, Gavin and Anthony to the closest exit. I strode up to Martin at the altar.

'Martin, go and get changed into your normal clothes. I'll wait for you here.'

Martin moved off straight away.

I stood at the altar, waiting. The murmurs in the church grew louder as every second passed. The gossip in Mildura had reached Red Cliffs. To the congregation, this was like watching a world title fight. It didn't come to blows. But I was not going to be stood over by this bastard priest. I turned and glared at him. He returned my stare with a look of shock and anger.

'You dirty bastard. You think I'm going to let you anywhere near my children?'

Day didn't say a word and returned his eyes to the congregation, attempting his most beneficent look, but I could tell he was rattled.

Martin appeared in his civvies a minute or two later. I grabbed his hand and walked towards Jean and the other three boys, who remained steadfast at the door. We got into the car and drove straight to Sacred Heart at Mildura, where we attended mass, knowing there was no likelihood of seeing Day there.

On the drive back to Red Cliffs, we saw Day driving his car, a late model Ford Fairlane, the other way along Eleventh Street. I don't know if he saw me. If he did, he didn't let on, but his hands were clenched tightly on the steering wheel and he had a look of impotent rage on his face.

So that was the last time I saw Monsignor John Day, but I would be dealing with ugly memories of him, his rape of children, and his bloated sense of entitlement and authority for many more years.

I remained very much alone in the police force during this period. I wondered if any copper would come forward with a promise to stand by me and give me a hand or some other form of moral support. Barritt, Irwin and McPartland were giving me a deluxe shafting. I needed the support of a genuine senior officer so I could continue with my investigation, or a senior investigator whom I could assist to be appointed. I decided to ring my old mate and mentor, Frank Holland, at that time a chief superintendent. Frank knew the score—he had helped me in past investigations when Barritt had stuck his bib in and nearly buggered things up.

'Frank, I've got a problem,' I told him. 'It's Barritt. I was conducting an inquiry into the local monsignor up here who is raping little kids. Barritt's jumped on it. It's come to a standstill and I've been ordered off the inquiry. Can you help me?'

'Yes, I know all about it,' Frank told me. 'Don't worry. Help is on its way.'

The help that was coming would be more of a hindrance, but it opened my eyes to the form and function of the Catholic Mafia in the Victoria Police force and the murky relationship it had with the Roman Catholic Church.

The help came in the form of John Quincy O'Connor, chief superintendent, chief investigator for the chief commissioner and the don of the Catholic Mafia.

John 'Baton Jack' O'Connor was not a physically imposing man. He was about my height, but his chief super's epaulets protruded under the force of his broad shoulders. He had a head of thick hair greying at the sides and the temples. He had perfected the long, uncomfortable, silent stare, and anyone who had ever engaged in conversation with him would remember O'Connor fixing his gaze on them.

Baton Jack got his nickname from his love of using a police issue baton as a tool of crisis management. A story often told in the police rumour mill was that, following a disagreement over a gambling debt, O'Connor beat an SP bookmaker's runner, or bet collector, to death at the CIB office at the old St Kilda police station. He then dragged the body out to his car and drove out to Centre Road, Bentleigh, where he dumped the body in the wee hours of the morning. O'Connor allegedly burnt some rubber around the runner's body to create the look of skid marks.

The Homicide Squad was called in. Detective Inspector Jack Ford, a close mate of O'Connor's, knew what to do. He wrote it up as a hit and run traffic incident, and naturally the crime remained unsolved. That was the rumour. I've spoken to a lot of police officers about this episode. Some believe it, others are less certain. O'Connor was capable of murder and Jack Ford was as corrupt as they come.

O'Connor was given the plum job of arresting the author Frank Hardy for criminal defamation in Hardy's book, *Power Without Glory*. The book had detailed the life of the illegal bookmaker and political puppetmaster, John Wren, and his close association with Archbishop Mannix. A bigoted Catholic like O'Connor would have enjoyed every minute of that arrest. The Catholic Church was his morning, noon and night.

O'Connor was a detective sergeant in Victoria's Special Branch, a clandestine group that saw reds under almost every bed. It was pro-Catholic and pro-Vatican, so there wasn't a Protestant in the place. Special Branch liaised closely with ASIO, sharing files and information. It also played an integral part in Australia's McCarthyite fight against the perceived threat of communism in Victoria. Following the Vatican's denunciation of communism in Pope Pius XI's encyclical in 1937, and the establishment of Special Branch in the period immediately after World War II, the branch became a virtual arm of the Catholic Church under the supervision of the archbishop of Melbourne, Daniel Mannix.

I'd met O'Connor back in the 1950s, when I was a detective in Melbourne. I'd been to his home in the eastern suburbs with Fred Russell. After O'Connor greeted us at the front door, Russell asked me to wait out on the street by the car. With me out of the way, the two men continued their conversation for twenty minutes. It was not until a year later that Russell asked me if I wanted to join the Catholic Mafia. But back then I wasn't in the fold. Perhaps I was being groomed to join up and that's why I was given the opportunity of a brief introduction to O'Connor.

I met O'Connor again in 1966, when I was in Mildura and he was district detective inspector (DDI). The DDI's position was considered a stepping stone to other more senior positions in the force. Once he'd had a quick look at the arrest book and our diaries, he grabbed me.

'Righto, Dinny,' he said. 'I'll tell Barritt that you're going to take me for a look around the district.'

I'd been warned about O'Connor. He had a huge appetite for the grog, and so it turned out. We spent the day in and around Mildura, drinking in pubs, and ended up blind drunk. All in a day's work.

'Bloody Masons have ruined the force,' he told me at one of our watering holes. 'When I make chief commissioner, that'll all change.'

A Catholic had never made it to the top in Victoria but O'Connor had the ambition and a talent for political intrigue that might just have taken him all the way.

The next time I saw O'Connor, he was standing in the lounge room of my home. It was the evening of 15 January 1972 and I'd just knocked off work. I'd seen the car in the driveway and wondered what was going on.

'G'day Dinny,' O'Connor said.

He was standing with Jean on one side and Detective Chief Inspector Harvey Child on the other. Child was a big bloke, well over 185 centimetres tall and heavily built. He'd spent time in the old Consorters, where he had developed a reputation for being a bit heavy-handed with the crims he kept tabs on. Perhaps he'd spent a bit too much time around these crims, because he looked like a thug. Harvey was also the brother of Ray Child, my old boss at Mordialloc. Ray didn't much care for his brother and had told me so.

'I don't trust Harvey and you shouldn't either if you ever come across him,' Ray had warned me.

Harvey was a rabid Freemason. He hated Catholics in the force and didn't think they belonged there. Anyone who was a Mason, however, got a rails run with Harvey.

Here was the help—a fervent Mason and a diabolically fanatical Catholic. I wondered why two senior policemen diametrically opposed philosophically and spiritually had been given carriage in this investigation. It turned out that Child was just along for the ride, a Mason to make up the numbers—window dressing, so that no one would question O'Connor having prejudiced the investigation by looking after his beloved Roman Catholic Church.

For serious matters, this was sometimes the way it was handled in the Victoria Police force. There'd be an officer from each team, Catholic or Freemason. And if the matter came before a court, the police would know if the judge was a Catholic or a Freemason, and the officers would offer evidence according to where the judge cut his lunch. Like meets like.

Child nodded in greeting. They'd been having a chat with Jean, nice and amiable.

'Can I have a word with you out the back?' O'Connor said. It was more of a command than a request.

I followed him out into the backyard. He kept walking until he found himself under an old peach tree.

'This is a nice old mess, Dinny.'

I didn't say anything, just waited for him to continue.

'What I intend to do is have Barritt moved on, and you will be made detective sergeant here,' he said.

The alarm bells started ringing straight away. There was no way I had the seniority for that position. Yes, O'Connor could have made it happen, but anyone with seniority who wanted the job could appeal. O'Connor's offer didn't ring true.

'I've done my sergeant's exam but I'd have to go back to Russell Street in uniform to be made a sergeant,' I said. 'Plus I've got my family settled here. My two oldest boys have asthma. They've improved up here, but until I get a medical clearance from their doctors, we have to stay. This position was given to me specifically for that reason by Superintendent Clugston. The doc says it might take a couple of years. I'd like to go back to Melbourne but I can't do it until the boys get the OK from the doc.'

'Don't worry about that, Dinny,' O'Connor replied with a grin. 'You won't be forced back to Melbourne until you want to go. Where there's a will, there's a way. I can make it all happen for you.'

Now the bells at Notre Dame were tolling in my ears.

'With due respect, sir,' I replied. 'It is not my intention to take Jim's position. I was asking for some assistance regarding the investigation into the crimes of Monsignor Day. Jim Barritt is too close to Day.'

'Dinny, we can smooth all this over,' he replied, still smiling.

'This goes back to my first day up here nine years ago. The first thing Jim did was take me up to the presbytery to meet Day. It was then that I realised I had met Day before. I was in the divisional van with Tommy Jenkins and Clarrie Bell in St Kilda back in 1956. We stopped Day with two prostitutes in Day's car. He was pissed to the eyeballs with his strides around his ankles. I didn't let on when I met Day, but I told

Jim after we left. He blew up, told me I was wrong and next thing I know Day has called me up to the presbytery where he shit-cans me and issues orders like he runs the town. It was a serious breach of trust by Jim, sir.'

'Dinny, Dinny . . .'

'Jim tried to tell me I had the wrong priest. He tried to tell me there was another Father Day in Apollo Bay. Day tried that one on, too. Jim completely lost me then. Sir, there is something sinister about their association.'

'Dinny, Barritt's gone. You'll be my man up here,' O'Connor said. 'But you have to play ball with me on this one.'

'I don't want Jim's job, sir. I want Day thoroughly investigated. He's an absolute disgrace to the priesthood and he should be unfrocked.'

The smile on O'Connor's face dropped.

'All right then,' he said, and walked back inside.

I remained under the peach tree for a moment. Jesus, did that just happen? O'Connor had just offered me a bribe. And I'd knocked it back. That meant I had a new enemy. And he was the biggest, baddest bastard in the force.

Before I regained my composure, O'Connor and Child came out again and walked passed me.

'I'll see you in the morning,' O'Connor said, his mood now sullen and bellicose.

The next day O'Connor blew into the office. I'd been waiting for his arrival with my heart in my mouth. I didn't know what to say to him. In the end, I didn't get a chance to say anything. He came over to my desk and told me he would be dealing with some business with the uniform boys and wouldn't get back to me about the Day investigation for another week.

He was off before I had a chance to say, 'Yes, sir.'

This left me in limbo yet again, with no support or anyone to turn to. At this time, the only advice I'd received on the conduct of the investigation was from Bishop Mulkearns. He knew more about it than I did.

A week later O'Connor came back up from Melbourne and breezed into the CIB office. He spent a lot of time in Barritt's office but I didn't know if Barritt was there or not; the door would always close behind O'Connor. His Mason partner, Harvey Child, was more or less invisible.

I sat at my desk, waiting for O'Connor to walk past so I could grab him and find out what was going on. He always made himself scarce, but one afternoon I saw him slip past and yelled out after him.

'Mr O'Connor, I would like to be part of the inquiry into Monsignor Day. As you know, sir, this was reported to me by the senior master at St Joseph's College as an official complaint from the principal of the school, Sister Pancratius. I've taken many statements. I can get a hundred more, sir.'

'No, you've been instructed that you're no longer part of this inquiry,' he replied firmly.

I tried again the following day.

'Mister O'Connor,' I said, jumping in his path while he walked down the corridor towards Barritt's office. 'I would like you to reconsider this. I have the local knowledge. I have the trust of the community. I can guarantee that I can find a hundred or more of Day's victims in this district alone.

God only knows how many more we could find in his other parishes.'

'You've been told once and so I'll tell you one more time,' O'Connor said, staring into my eyes. 'You are not involved in this investigation. You've been issued a direct order and if you don't obey it, you will be subject to disciplinary action.'

That was it. I was out. O'Connor didn't mention the Day investigation to me again until he interviewed me in Melbourne a month later.

Just to prove a point, I obtained a further statement from another of Day's victims, who had been sexually assaulted when he was 11 years of age. His statement refers to an episode in 1956, when he had been unfortunate enough to win the vaulting competition at Sacred Heart Primary School under the watchful eye of Day. His prize was a week away with Day, who sexually assaulted the boy in two separate incidents.

There would always be more evidence to obtain, and even after I left the force victims came forward to tell me their stories. Others came through the grapevine. There were dozens in Mildura, some from Apollo Bay, some from Day's time at Horsham. Hundreds of victims in total, as I had thought.

The best thing I had done was to drag Day kicking and screaming out of the muck and into the light, with Barritt and Kearney following afterwards. People in Mildura were now willing to speak up. The great shame of it was that no one in authority was listening.

Day, Barritt and Kearney would all fall from grace but not one of them was ever brought to account in a courtroom— not Barritt, for his corruption and prior knowledge of Day's outrages; not Kearney, for his fraud and his rape of a young woman; and not Day, the third and highest member of the unholy trinity, for his crimes against children. The triumvirate was collapsing, disintegrating at a rapid rate of knots.

Kearney was the first to go. He never got pulled up for raping that young woman in his office, but he left town in a hurry after his fraud came to the attention of the Crown Law Department in 1971. The court's accounts were audited. Money was missing here, there and everywhere. He'd been threatened with a jail term if he didn't move along and keep his mouth shut. I didn't even know he was gone until someone told me he'd cleaned his desk out and was headed down to Melbourne. The last I heard he was pushing a pencil at the Springvale courthouse. Maybe he just kept his head down after his crimes in Mildura.

On 28 January 1972, O'Connor and Child met up with John Howden and the builder Terry Lynch at the Grand Hotel in Mildura. John and Terry sat waiting for O'Connor and Child, who turned up on the dot of five o'clock and bought a round of beers.

O'Connor spoke first. 'We're driving down now to see Bishop Mulkearns in Ballarat. We're going to tell him to remove Day from Mildura or we'll charge him.'

'Day's gone. He's either out of Mildura or in jail,' Child chipped in.

The two senior coppers finished their beers and took off. Howden and Lynch sat there, gobsmacked, but were happy that Day's reign in Mildura was coming to an end.

But the burning question remained—why wouldn't Day be charged immediately, or at the very least further inquiries made?

Later that day O'Connor and Child met with Bishop Ronald Mulkearns. With Joe Kearney out of action, the flow of information to the diocese came to a halt. Mulkearns hadn't heard the latest development. He greeted O'Connor and Child with a haughty dismissal of the allegations against Day, assuming the whole dirty business had been resolved by Irwin and Barritt's joke of an investigation. O'Connor told him there was more and proceeded to reel off the list of statements that I had obtained in December and January.

Mulkearns dropped his defence of Day. At least it was all over for the people of Mildura, and Day was summoned to appear before the bishop the following afternoon.

At mass on Sunday, 30 January, Monsignor John Day informed the congregation that he had offered his resignation to Bishop Mulkearns. It had been accepted, and Day would be leaving the parish within days. The congregation erupted into murmurs. Still divided, some believed Day had been poorly treated. Others were glad to see the back of him.

Barritt, too, was in plenty of strife. He was under an internal investigation for extorting money from the two blokes who had received the hot outboard motor and been told by Barritt to slip a hundred each into the Sacred Heart building fund.

Not that I knew any of this at the time. No one was talking to me. O'Connor, Child, Barritt and Irwin were all lying doggo. In Swan Hill, Superintendent Jack McPartland had been transferred back to Melbourne. His replacement, Superintendent Harry Duffy, had written to Chief Commissioner Reg Jackson recommending my transfer, but I didn't know about that then either.

In the meantime, Irwin had pulled me up. He told me he had received an order from Jackson and I was forbidden to leave the district without Irwin's permission. It was an unusual instruction to say the least. In fact, it was unheard of, and later, when I told senior police officers, they would shake their heads in disbelief.

There I was, not quite restricted to barracks but put on a short leash. Jackson was aware that I had obtained further statements and was making further inquiries. I was a loose cannon that had to be secured to the decks. But O'Connor was the architect. He was the master of political intrigue, and he knew exactly what had gone on. It was very messy, and only a cunning strategist like O'Connor could find a path through the mire. He had convinced Mulkearns that Day had to be removed. O'Connor also had to get rid of Barritt. After I'd knocked back O'Connor's offer to give me Barritt's job, I'd have to be cut adrift, too.

O'Connor's scheme would spare the Catholic Church its precious reputation, but I suspect he was more interested in the good name of the Victoria Police force and, by extension, his own arse. If Day had been charged, it would expose Barritt and, if Barritt was exposed, then the entire Catholic Mafia was vulnerable. No, Day had to walk away. Barritt had to be transferred. Joe Kearney had to be pushed out. Kearney couldn't be charged either, or the entire bucket of shit could come tumbling down on them all. Another transfer. Out of sight, out of mind.

Me? Well, O'Connor's inducement hadn't worked the first time around but O'Connor remained hopeful. The soft touch hadn't worked, so now it was time for the blowtorch on my belly. O'Connor had no doubt I'd see the error of my ways, by hook or by crook.

It was the perfect solution. Protect the Catholic Church and establish a level of deniability around the senior ranks of the Victoria Police force. Two birds, one stone. That just left Day's victims, and what voice did they have?

O'Connor's report to Deputy Commissioner Jack Carmichael indicated that he had interviewed some of the twelve victims from whom I had obtained statements. I found only one victim who had been contacted by O'Connor. He told me that O'Connor had tried to stand over him, but he wouldn't be intimidated and stuck by his story. Neither O'Connor nor Child had been within a bull's roar of the other eleven victims. No interviews, no cursory inquiry. Not so much as a phone call.

On the day before he left the Mildura parish for the last time, Monsignor Day was seen down at the Mildura tip, among an acre of household detritus. He had a fire going and was flinging documents on to the flames. It was the 1972 equivalent of paper shredding. Every dirty, incriminating little piece of paper had to be destroyed.

He had outlived his welcome in Mildura but Monsignor Day was off the hook. He was driving down to Melbourne for a few weeks before heading overseas. He'd been given a world tour for his crimes—a trip to Chicago followed by a stint in Portugal for 'counselling'. All expenses paid.

When all the fuss died down, he'd head back to Victoria where he'd be sent to a new parish. Life for a disgraced priest wasn't too bad after all.

8

A BRUSH WITH SCANDAL

*In a time of universal deceit,
telling the truth is a revolutionary act.*
GEORGE ORWELL, 1903–1950

The member for Midlands, Les Shilton, got to his feet in the lower house of the Victorian Parliament. It was question time in the Legislative Assembly. Shilton had been a senior detective at Seymour before becoming a Labor politician, elected to the parliament in 1970.

Hansard records that, on 7 March 1972, Shilton addressed a question to the then chief secretary and deputy premier, Rupert Hamer: 'Will the Chief Secretary advise the House of the result of the investigation conducted quite recently by two senior officers into the police administration in Mildura.'

Hamer replied: 'No doubt the honourable member is referring to the complaint alleged against one member of the Victoria Police force stationed at Mildura. This matter has been investigated by two senior officers of the force in accordance with the custom.'

An interjection from Opposition leader, Frank Wilkes, is recorded: 'They were not very senior.'

'They were fairly senior,' Hamer responded. 'They were the usual ones. I understand their report is before the Chief Commissioner at present. I have not seen it but I will inform the Honourable Member of the result as soon as I can.'

It's interesting that Hamer was all over this so early, but then he would be. As chief secretary, a cabinet position that is now long gone, he was the state's principal administrator and oversaw most of Victoria's bureaucracy, including police matters. Like all smart politicians, he had a sixth sense for detecting scandal. And scandal was coming. As a senior member of the government, Hamer understood this. He'd already apprised himself of the rough facts of the case before Shilton had asked his question.

The premier, Sir Henry Bolte, had held the reins for eighteen years, but the 1970 election had been a close call for the Liberal government. People had grown tired of Bolte's rough and tumble politics. Labor had been tipped to win the election but the left-wing faction of the party had stuffed it up. An internal dispute over funding for non-government schools had cost Wilkes the government.

The Liberal Party knew Bolte had to go, and a smooth transition had been lined up. Reluctantly, the hardliner Bolte was passing the baton to the moderate Hamer, who had made the move from the Legislative Council to the Legislative Assembly the year before. From the vegetables to the animals, so to speak. It had all been planned.

Hamer had been in parliament for fifteen years. He could sniff the wind. He knew this scandal had the power to bring the government down or see it slaughtered at the ballot box. A priest raping children, protected by elements of the police force—where would that end?

Despite O'Connor's best efforts to smother the case and thwart the investigation into Day, there were some loose ends. And I was loose end number one.

Shilton was on my side. I'd been introduced to him by Alan Lind, the member for Dandenong. Jack Leary, a rusted-on Labor man and a committee member at the Working Man's Club, teed it all up. Jack was the manager of the dried fruit packing sheds and one of the few people in Mildura who had offered me any support.

I travelled to Melbourne by train to meet Lind. I was still under orders not to leave the district, but I tippy-toed away. Lind then introduced me to Shilton, whose years of experience as a police officer ensured he would be my contact within parliament. He understood police procedures and the way a police officer thought. It was a good fit. We spoke for about an hour and Les took some notes.

I told him everything I knew. Day, Barritt, Kearney, Irwin, McPartland, O'Connor and Child. I told him about pulling up Day in St Kilda in 1956. I told him about the victims in Mildura, and how many other victims I thought there might have been. Even as a hardened ex-copper, Shilton struggled to comprehend the extent of it. That evening I left his office knowing that I had someone in my corner who could pack a punch.

I was on my own in Mildura, but I had to do something. I could have drip fed information to the media but I refused to do so. The meeting with Shilton had enabled me to get my story into the public arena. I wasn't interested in turning it into a circus.

When Les asked his question in parliament on 7 March, Hamer was one short step ahead, but he knew that the Opposition had someone on the inside. I suppose the government would have understood it was me. It wouldn't have been hard to work out the arithmetic on that one.

The government would have its quid pro quo. A few days after I returned to Mildura I was called into Irwin's office.

'I need you to be my driver on a licensing matter tomorrow. It'll take all day.'

'Now, hang on. I'm not a driver. I've got nothing to do with licensing matters. Why don't you get one of the uniform branch to drive you?'

'I'm issuing you with a direct order and I expect you to obey it. Do you understand?'

You're a shifty bastard, Alby, I thought. What are you up to now?

'All right. What time tomorrow?'

'Eight-thirty on the dot,' Irwin replied. That was all he had to say. He put his head down and stared rummaging through some papers on his desk. I got the message and marched off.

The following day, Irwin and I headed out of Mildura with me at the wheel. It was a blazing hot morning. The mercury would nudge 42 degrees later in the afternoon. I had hoped the excursion would thaw the iciness that had characterised our relationship for the previous six months, but every time I attempted to strike up a conversation Irwin sat silent and sullen next to me. Nothing doing. Permafrost.

We drove down the Calder Highway into Ouyen.

'Where to now?' I asked.

'Keep driving,' Irwin said.

That was all he said to me until we drove into the hamlet of Berriwillock—just a roadhouse with a town sign out the front.

'Pull over in front of the store here,' Irwin said.

I parked the unmarked police car alongside the roadhouse.

'I'm going inside,' Irwin said, getting out of the car. 'You wait here.'

I waited, sweating like a bastard in the car. I considered getting out and going inside but thought I'd be better off playing Irwin's game. So I waited a bit more, sweltering in the car, from time to time turning the engine on to get the air conditioning running. Three hours after I pulled up at the roadhouse, Irwin came out looking refreshed, fed and watered. He got back into the car.

'Right. Back to Mildura,' Irwin said.

'I'll stop at Ouyen and get something to eat and drink, if you don't mind,' I said.

It was past lunchtime. I was hungry and after sitting in the car in the hot sun all that time, I had a thirst that could be rendered in oil.

'No,' Irwin replied. 'Drive straight through.'

I couldn't be bothered arguing. I started the engine and turned the car around for the drive back to Mildura.

We got back just after five o'clock. I parked the car. Irwin went in his way, through the front door of the police station. I went through the CIB entrance.

I walked past Bill Brodie. He looked at me.

'Don't ask,' I told him. 'I've had a shit of a day.'

I made my way to my desk. Brodie came over.

'Barritt's down in Melbourne,' Brodie said, almost in a whisper. 'He flew down this morning. He's meeting Under Secretary Dillon.'

I sighed. Before I could look up, Brodie had gone back to Barritt's office. Within minutes I heard the CIB door close. He'd gone for the day.

I went to the tearoom and gulped down four glasses of water. I'd better look into this, I thought. I gave the Qantas booking office a call. They confirmed Barritt had left Mildura on the first flight to Melbourne that morning and was due to return later that night.

What had Barritt been up to, visiting Dillon? Sir John Vincent Dillon was a very powerful man. A devout Catholic, the under secretary was the most senior bureaucrat in the state. Maybe Brodie had the story wrong.

I rang Alan Lind down in Melbourne. Did he know of the meeting? He told me he would make a few discreet inquiries. He rang me back within an hour.

'Your mate Barritt was with Dillon this afternoon,' he told me.

It all made sense. Irwin had to get me out of the station for the day. That's why I'd spent the day in the car on the verge of dehydration and heat exhaustion. Barritt had flown down to meet Dick Hamer's right-hand man. If I had fed information to the Opposition, then the government needed some background on me.

Dillon could have asked anyone in the force—O'Connor, Jackson, Carmichael. Any of the bigwigs in Russell Street. Dillon knew that Barritt and I were at loggerheads. And he figured that if anyone was going to have dirt on me, it would be Barritt. The government was preparing my dossier. If this blew up, they could fling out shit sheets to the media. Not quite shooting the messenger, but loading the bullets and handing the gun to the press.

Not that they had much. Barritt was flailing about, trying to dig up some dirt. He regarded my amateur theatrical performances as an affectation. He put two and two together in his malicious addle-headed way and came up with five. He started telling anyone who cared to listen—and by this stage there weren't many—that I was a homosexual. No doubt he imparted this to Dillon. I don't know what Dillon would have made of the connection, but the fact that I was married with four children would have rendered the allegation unlikely.

Meanwhile, the puppet master 'Baton Jack' O'Connor had been busy. He and Child went to St James Presbytery in Elsternwick, a sort of halfway house for displaced priests, to interview Monsignor Day on 2 March. Day had been putting his feet up there while he prepared for his overseas jaunt.

The die had been cast. This was no milk run. The puppet master and his assistant made it clear to Day that they had him on toast. In a sense they were exacting some element of revenge. Not for the victims; for them, retribution would never come. But O'Connor and Child wanted to make Day squirm. He was the bastard who had created this problem—bringing the Church into disrepute, and threatening the police force with scandal, shame and the exposure of corruption. Commissions of inquiry. Cops in the witness stand; some frogmarched off to jail. It was bad for business. If only Day had kept his dick in his trousers.

This would be no easy interview, with the questions prepared and handed to him in advance as Irwin and Barritt had done. O'Connor and Child got out the blowtorch and pliers. Child asked the questions. It was better that way. O'Connor, the dyed-in-the-wool Catholic, might have been inclined to go easy on Day. The record of interview shows that Day did squirm. At first he babbled that his lawyer had instructed him not to answer any questions, but Child and O'Connor made it clear that strategy was not going to wash.

Child and O'Connor stood over him, and Child gave him the third degree. They put him in his place, made him appreciate that they knew what he'd been up to. They pushed Day to breaking point. They told him they had the corroboration they needed. It was the only time Day started to really sweat.

Day rounded on his parishioners. He blamed the people he had served for his problems. He referred to one parishioner as a drunk, another as a harlot. There were broken homes and idle, sinful parents, he said. Howden and I had engineered an intricate conspiracy to remove him from Mildura. It was all somebody else's fault.

Still, the confession did not come. A psychopath like Day would never throw his hands up. Instinctively, he knew they weren't going to charge him. He knew they knew about his crimes, but they didn't want a confession. That would have buggered things right up. So he remained staunch. O'Connor and Child were impressed. But knowing that they knew what he had done was enough. Having his dog collar threatened was a powerful motivator. Day now belonged to them.

At the end of the interview, the rattled priest asked: 'Am I still allowed to go on my overseas trip?'

'Monsignor, ten thousand miles from Mildura is the best place for you to be,' O'Connor said. 'You can spend the rest of your life overseas as far as I care. If you're going to come back, make sure it's not soon.'

And that was that. Day knew he was going to walk. There would be no further investigations. The smother was almost complete.

I had a formal interview with O'Connor myself around the same time. Not that it lasted long.

I was the only fly left in the ointment. The smother would not work if I could not be pulled into line. The bullshit started flying around. I would be accused of moonlighting, because I owned the orchard and made a few quid out of the fruit. My accountant told me I was earning twenty dollars a week out of it, maybe enough to buy a bag of groceries in 1972.

That was about all they could find, and they couldn't make even that stick. I had a clean record in the force. Distinctions, chief commissioner's certificate, thirteen commendatory entries on my file. I was respected and well liked in the community. A group of prominent citizens had written to the chief commissioner, stating that any attempt to transfer me would be 'tantamount to a condemnation of [my] part in the investigations'. It was only years later that I discovered they had sent the letter, in spite of my urging them not to.

It was a very nice gesture on the part of these people but it didn't amount to much.

O'Connor dug deep but he had nothing. Or almost nothing.

He summoned me to Melbourne. Irwin had passed the message on—get down to Melbourne, O'Connor wants to see you. Before I was due to go in and prostrate myself before

O'Connor, I met a mate of mine at the Transport Branch, across the road from police headquarters. My mate knew O'Connor and his methods. He was a surveillance expert in the Bureau of Criminal Intelligence.

'I'll give you some mail on O'Connor,' he told me. 'Just watch him when you sit down. If his hand goes down to the right and he pulls his second desk drawer open slightly, it will activate a tape recorder. From that time on everything you say will be taped.'

'How do you know that?' I asked.

'I installed it.'

There was no waiting in the anteroom for O'Connor. I was called into his office at eleven o'clock sharp, as directed. I stood in front of him.

'Take a seat,' O'Connor said. The amiable camaraderie he'd shown at my place in Mildura a month before was all gone. I'd knocked him back then. Now it was strictly business, by the numbers. I sat down and watched O'Connor drop his right arm down and pull at his desk drawer before meeting my eye.

'Is this conversation going to be taped?' I asked.

'No, it's not,' he replied in a cold-blooded fashion.

'I advise you now that I do not consent to this interview being taped,' I told him. 'If I discover that the interview is taped without my permission, I will seek legal redress.'

Our eyes locked for a moment before O'Connor closed the drawer. A long silence ensued, then O'Connor cleared his throat.

'I am advising you that you will be charged with failing to complete the outcome of an arrest in your CIB diary.'

'You have got to be joking. There wouldn't be a detective in the state you couldn't charge with that. And that includes yourself.'

'That will be all, detective.'

I got up and walked out. It was a try on, an effort to intimidate me. If I wouldn't play ball, O'Connor was going to play hardball.

O'Connor's report to the chief commissioner was a knockout job, prepared and sent to his office two days after Shilton had posed the question to the government. O'Connor concurred with Superintendent Duffy and Irwin that the 'evidence is insufficient to prosecute Monsignor Day'. The report was wending its way around the third floor of Russell Street—first to Chief Commissioner Jackson, then Deputy Commissioner Jack Carmichael and Under Secretary Dillon, and finally to Hamer in the parliament.

On 29 March Barritt and I were called to Russell Street to meet the bigwigs, Jackson and Carmichael.

Barritt and I waited outside Jackson's office, glaring at each other. He went in first and closed the door behind him. He emerged about half an hour later, solemn and serious. He walked straight by me.

It was my turn.

'All right,' Jackson said, after I sat down. 'Why can't you get on with Jim Barritt? What are the problems you've got with him?'

It was hard to know where to begin. I told Jackson and Carmichael that Barritt's brother Dinny had warned me about him before I transferred to Mildura. I told them about Barritt taking me to see Day on my first day of duty in Mildura, and how Barritt had ranted and raved when I told him about pulling up Day in St Kilda, and how I was concerned that Barritt had breached a confidence in informing Day of my recollections. I told them about Barritt's inadequacies as a detective.

I went on for a good ten minutes. Jackson and Carmichael only interrupted me when I mentioned Barritt by name but without noting his rank.

'That's Detective Sergeant Barritt to you,' Carmichael tut-tutted.

'Show some respect for your senior officer,' Jackson admonished.

'He might be my senior officer but he's a dangerous fool.'

They let me go on. When I stopped to draw breath Jackson looked up.

'That will be all, detective.'

Carmichael had his head down and Jackson started scratching away with a pen on a notepad. The meeting was over. I got up and walked out.

The investigation into Day didn't get a mention. Jackson and Carmichael had already made up their minds about that. The priest was off the hook. O'Connor had made that problem go away. Priests raping kids was low on their scale of priorities. The issue had been reduced to one of a police station feud between Barritt and me.

With Day elbowed out of the way, there was no way he'd turn on O'Connor now. He had far too much to lose.

O'Connor and Child had Barritt banged to rights, just where they wanted him. He'd been put under the microscope over extorting money from the two blokes who'd fallen foul of him over the hot outboard motor. They could bring

Barritt before a police disciplinary hearing. He might have been threatened with criminal charges. He would go quietly.

A few months earlier, when Barritt was in the gun from O'Connor and looking at a transfer, he had solicited half a dozen references from Mildurans. The letters, all in pro forma type, were sent to the chief commissioner. But they didn't do that pudding-headed bastard any good.

For O'Connor, Barritt was the crucial figure. If push came to shove, Barritt could prove to be the weak link in the chain. O'Connor knew he'd protected Day and that he had known of Day's crimes against children. Barritt was a made man in the Catholic Mafia. If Day went down, he could drag Barritt down with him and, if that happened, O'Connor and the Catholic Mafia would all be in the shit. Barritt had to be kept sweet—and he would be.

Assistant Commissioner Bill Crowley covered for Barritt in a report to Chief Commissioner Jackson, smoothing the waters. The report read in part: 'Having had the opportunity of examining this file and discussing this matter on several occasions with Chief Superintendent O'Connor and Detective Chief Inspector Child, it is my view that no further action, disciplinary or otherwise, should be taken against Detective Sergeant Barritt. Despite his well known deficiencies, in my opinion Barritt is a completely honest and incorruptible member of the force whose integrity I would accept in any situations [sic]. I sincerely believe that the humiliation that he is undoubtedly suffering is more than sufficient punishment.'

Barritt did not know he had so many senior officers in his corner. If he had, he would have fought like hell to stay in Mildura.

Barritt had told O'Connor he didn't want to go back to Melbourne. He liked it up on the Murray River. If he couldn't stay at Mildura, was there another job going somewhere on the river?

There wasn't, but that didn't matter. For his silence, co-operation and service beyond the call of duty to the Catholic Mafia, a position was created for him at Echuca, 400 kilometres upstream. It was the VicPol equivalent of the golden parachute. His reputation preceded him.

And this useless, corrupt policeman, as good as a man short, remained a detective sergeant in the Victoria Police force. A detective mate of mine who was unfortunate enough to be stationed there with him, later told me Barritt was 'the greatest bastard I've ever worked with'.

Another detective Barritt had worked with gave me a bell when this whole business was blowing up. His wife had been on close terms with Barritt's wife, Alma.

'I hear you're having a rough time up there,' the detective told me on the phone.

'You can say that again,' I replied.

'This might help you,' he said. 'Barritt's a very strange fish. I was stationed up there years ago with him. His wife told my missus that she'd never seen Jim naked. He used to strip off at night in the bathroom. She told her that he had never consummated the marriage. Never gave his missus one once.'

'I know. He's an unusual man,' I told him.

'Well, now you know he's a bit more unusual than you'd thought.'

The child pornography in his desk drawer. The complaints from the magistrate, Joe Hayes, that Barritt took unnecessarily lurid statements from young women. Barritt's friendship with Day. I'm no shrink but there's enough there for an entire seminar on abnormal psychology.

Barritt faced disciplinary charges over demanding money from the two truckers. It was the least of his crimes at Mildura. And he walked away with a slap on the wrist. His brother Dinny, the man who had warned me about him, had become a barrister and represented his pudding-headed brother.

Dinny would go on to become the coroner in the Azaria Chamberlain death. He handed his findings down in 1981. He got it right: the dingo did it. But the media ignored him and so the circus began.

Jim Barritt—the corrupt detective, covert ASIO operative, embellisher of his war record and bane of my existence—retired from the force after eight more years in Echuca. I never caught sight of him after he left Mildura. One must be thankful for small mercies.

A former police officer from the other side of the Murray told me that Barritt and some dodgy race track pimp he was knocking around with had tried to rig a horse race at Broken Hill. A ring-in had been planned. Barritt thought the ex-copper might be a willing accomplice but he knocked Barritt back. I don't know if the ring-in ever took place but I've never had a bet at the Broken Hill races just in case. Barritt died in 1997.

If the smother was going to work, I had to be transferred, too. I knew that when I walked out of Jackson's office. I'd thought I was facing the prospect of a transfer for the previous few months. The meeting with Jackson and Carmichael merely confirmed it. I had told O'Connor that a transfer back to Melbourne could put my two eldest boys' health at risk, but that didn't matter to O'Connor or Jackson or Carmichael.

If I remained in Mildura, they feared I would continue the investigation into Day. They got that right. I had told O'Connor I could get a hundred statements. I was convinced of that. The further I went with the investigation, the more certain I became. So they had to get me out.

Carmichael's report didn't deal with the investigation of Day at all. It was all brought down to the level of my feud with Barritt. I got hold of a copy of the report many years later. It dealt in large part with the allegations against Barritt and the backhanders he'd demanded over the stolen outboard motor.

I got a mention for my property and the orchard, from which I made a pittance. Carmichael declared that the 'nature and scope of this business interest is considered to conflict too sharply with his primary role as a member of the force leading to a situation where his divided interests adversely affect his work performance'.

A twenty dollar a week business. Neither Carmichael nor Jackson had raised it with me. It was a fit-up. It was the only thing they had and it would never stand up to scrutiny. Just like O'Connor telling me I was going to be charged for failing to make an entry in my detective's diary. And just like O'Connor's threat, it came to nothing.

And finally, Carmichael demonstrated a streak of sympathy, albeit in a backhanded fashion.

'At first sight it would appear unfair to Senior Detective Ryan that he should be directed to transfer, for it was information supplied by him that led to the disclosure of events at Mildura. Nevertheless, as the subsequent inquiry brought his own position in the matter under scrutiny, factors of his involvement cannot be disregarded when administrative solutions to the problem are being sought.'

It was a textbook example of bureaucratese. Blather replacing facts.

Carmichael's report followed O'Connor's. In it he said that he 'strongly suspected that many of Barritt's difficulties have been aggravated by Senior Detective Ryan's lack of co-operation'.

So I was out. It was my punishment for the offence of trying to bring a paedophile priest to account. The orders came through and I was required to report to Russell Street CIB on 22 May 1972. To them, it didn't matter if I was in Russell Street or on the dark side of the moon. They just wanted me out of Mildura. I received notice of the transfer on 12 April when I was in my office. Irwin came walking in.

'I have received notification from the commissioner's office that you are to be transferred out of Mildura. You can apply for any station that is available by the fifteenth of May but if you have made no application then you will be transferred to Russell Street CIB.'

Irwin marched off. I didn't say a word. Even though I'd been expecting it for months, the transfer order left me shocked and bitterly disappointed.

I was determined to appeal, but in order to do so I needed the support of the Police Association—the trade union of the police force. The Police Association would hear my story and if they thought I had been poorly treated, they would find the best barrister to argue my case at the Police Appeals Board, all free of charge to me.

I rang an official at the association and made an appointment to see him. I was still confined to the district by order of Irwin, so I had to get his permission before I made the trip. I told him I was going to appeal the decision to have me transferred out of Mildura and seek the support and the assistance of the association. He grunted his acceptance and I booked a ticket on the train to Melbourne. I didn't know this at the time, but while I was doing so, Irwin was on the phone to O'Connor. O'Connor wasn't going to let my appeal get up. He'd make a few phone calls and make sure the appeal wouldn't get off the ground.

Back then the Police Association office was in MacKenzie Street, in the shadow of Russell Street headquarters. I made my way from Spencer Street along to the office where a receptionist ushered me in to see the official. I introduced myself to the official and put my hand out in greeting. He stood up but didn't shake my hand, even though I continued to hold out mine. He then resumed his seat and, taking his prompt, I sat down in front of him.

'How can I help you?' he asked.

'I want to appeal my transfer from Mildura CIB to Russell Street.'

I started telling him the whole story. I detailed my investigation of Day and how that had begun with a call from John Howden. I told him that I had interviewed Day's victims, who had all provided me with signed statements.

The official seemed to be taking this all in his stride, nodding occasionally or shaking his head in a show of empathy.

I was about to tell him that O'Connor offered me the bribe in the backyard of my home when the official suddenly rose from his chair and took off out of the office and down the corridor, yelling, 'This is too much for me! I can't handle this!'

I was startled by his reaction but I remained in his office, sitting patiently, hoping he would soon recover his composure and return. I sat there for half an hour before I realised he was probably not going to come back. I got up and approached the receptionist.

'Do you think he'll be back at all today?' I asked.

'I wouldn't think so,' she replied apologetically.

That was my last contact with the Police Association. I got on the train and went back to Mildura. I rang the official and left five or six messages but he never got back to me.

That was my last avenue of appeal gone. I could have appealed the transfer myself or engaged a solicitor, but I didn't have two bob to rub together. No, I was gone. I'd been stitched up by experts.

Now I was faced with a real dilemma. I didn't know what to do. I could bow to the dictates of O'Connor and the Catholic Mafia and allow another Catholic priest to join the army of priests who have escaped the clutches of the law for committing the most heinous of crimes against young children. This would mean going back to Russell Street under the thumb of the Catholic Mafia.

But Jean and I had continuing concerns regarding the health of our two eldest boys. A return to Melbourne could trigger further asthma attacks. Certainly, their doctor believed it was possible. Most importantly, if I transferred, it would mean that the investigation into Day would end once and for all. My obligation to the victims who had come forward, to the many who had not, and also to the other children who would fall prey to his depravity will weigh on my mind until the day I die.

If I resigned from the force and stayed in Mildura, my voice would still be heard, but I would lose my pension and all my benefits. I had twenty years' service in the police force; the qualification for the super scheme for police and emergency service workers was thirty years. If I took the sergeant's position, I would be throwing all that away—more than $300,000 at my current rank—and much more. I'd walk away with little more than long service leave of three months, plus my police pension as it stood after twenty years. It amounted to a tick over $4000. I'd have to get a job. Our little orchard could not support the family, despite what O'Connor and Carmichael may have insinuated.

The police force had been my life and I was being driven out of it. Being a police officer was in my DNA. Even after all these years, I still think like a policeman and miss the mateship and the thrill of the hunt.

It was 1972. No Catholic priest had ever been charged with child sexual abuse; it was unheard of. In 1978, Michael Glennon, a Catholic priest, would be the first cleric to go before the courts. Glennon was a maverick, and after his first conviction the Church cut him loose. It would be the best part of twenty years before Gerald Ridsdale was convicted, with the Church kicking and screaming every step of the way. That fact reveals the extent and the effectiveness of the cover up. I had seen it at first hand with Day. I had no idea of the real power of the Catholic Mafia, but what I had seen had been deplorable. Walking away from the investigation of Day meant the bad guys would win and the Roman Catholic Church had learnt nothing.

Only my family and my God would ever really appreciate the anguish and abiding sense of hopelessness I experienced during that time.

❖

I decided to walk after I got the formal order to transfer from the new superintendent, Bill McBride. I sent off a report to him, stating that the pressure that Irwin and Barritt had brought to bear on me since I had started investigating Day had left me with no other option than to offer my resignation. I rounded off the letter by stating that I hoped no other detective would have to suffer what I had in merely doing my duty.

I went on sick leave. I was in a bleak mood, depressed and bitter. I did my best to conceal it from the boys. Jean and I had discussed my options. Like me, she was down in the dumps. Now we also had money worries. Our happy household had been thrown into doubt and fear of the future.

McBride rang Red Cliffs police station and ordered a uniform constable to get out to my house with specific instructions for me to call him as soon as possible.

I drove into the station and grabbed a phone.

'It's Denis Ryan ringing. I got a message to call you.'

'How dare you submit a resignation like this?' McBride thundered down the line. 'You can be charged with insubordination. You could be dismissed from the police force. Sacked. And you would not receive a penny. I am now demanding that you withdraw this resignation and submit an acceptable one.'

'My resignation stands. You do what you bloody well like,' I told McBride, and hung the phone up in his ear.

I sat there for a while, contemplating my next move. I didn't have too many options left. I was gone. No longer Detective Senior Constable Denis James Henry Ryan No. 11468 of the Victoria Police force. I was just another bloke on the street.

Day, Barritt, Irwin, O'Connor—the whole bloody lot of them—had won. Alby Irwin—that scared, timid excuse of a police officer—was promoted to chief inspector. He got a pass out of Mildura to sit on the Police Disciplinary Board in Melbourne. As O'Connor's gravy train was leaving the station, Irwin jumped on board.

In the middle of this fog of intrigue, even I was starting to lose sight of what this had been all about—the victims. I had been the collateral damage in O'Connor's smother, but Day's victims had lost more than me. They had lost the opportunity to receive justice, to see their tormentor standing in disgrace in the dock. They had learnt that the Catholic Church cared nothing for their pain and that the police would do nothing to prevent Day from committing further acts of sexual violence against children.

The smother had been effective. On 17 April the Victorian Crown Law Department provided advice to Under Secretary Dillon, confirming the assertions of O'Connor and of Irwin and Barritt—that there was insufficient evidence to prosecute Day. The report in part stated the obvious: 'I trust the authorities in the Church will realise that the decision not to prosecute does not arise from any conviction that the allegations are unfounded. Having regard to the similarities of the various accounts, there would appear to be little doubt that Day misconducted himself.'

I'd taken twelve statements from Day's victims, all alleging that he had raped and subjected them to gross indecencies. The allegations ran across thirteen years. I hadn't touched on Day's time at Colac, Apollo Bay, Beech Forest, Horsham, Ararat or Ballarat East. The victims I'd found had all been in Mildura—altar boys, gymnasts, and boys and girls at the Sacred Heart Primary School and St Joseph's College.

The upper echelons of the police and our criminal justice system claimed that not only was there insufficient evidence to convict, but also that no further investigation would take place. That was how well O'Connor's smother had worked.

The bigwigs of the commissariat at Russell Street headquarters were placated. The good name of the Victoria Police force would not be tarnished. The Catholic Mafia would not be exposed. The reputation of the Catholic Church would not be sullied. The government was satisfied. The scandal had passed. The twelve statements I had taken were left to rot in the bowels of the force's file repositories in a gigantic warehouse in Melbourne's western suburbs.

So many questions remained. Not the least of all was—what might happen to Day's victims?

❖

Later in 1972, Day returned from his overseas trip, refreshed and raring to go. He had spent weeks in Chicago, staying in the finest hotels before travelling to Portugal and putting on his most convincing penitent face for his counselling sessions. He had a great deal to be penitent for—nearly half a century of abusing and raping children. Hundreds of victims and tens of thousands of offences.

The Catholic Church had learnt nothing from the experience. The same old techniques remained in place. Bishop Mulkearns dispatched Day to Timboon, a tiny parish 50 kilometres east of Warrnambool. Another town in western Victoria to take on a priest with a dark, sinister past; another parish deceived; another unsuspecting community; another group of unwary children.

Day was active in the parish and wandered around, in his dotage by then, without any restrictions. He could take the mass. He was not prevented from being in contact with children. The people of Timboon had no idea of Day's sordid history. He remained there until his death in 1978, at 74 years of age. He had been a priest and an active paedophile for forty-eight years. When he died, he was feted by the Catholic Church. Bishop Mulkearns praised Day in the eulogy, describing his 'humble magnificence'. Mulkearns depicted Day as 'impetuous, flamboyant and a lover of great occasions but also proved himself capable of relentless work and unresting zeal'. Of his time in Mildura, Mulkearns mentioned Day's 'great work in extending and refurnishing the parish church in Mildura'.

Part of the eulogy was republished in the September 1978 edition of *The Light*, the journal of the Ballarat diocese. The journal editorialised: 'Nor was there anything narrow or parochial about [Day]. He involved the parish community in the work of the civic community and gave it a sense of identity stronger than it ever was before.'

Bishop Mulkearns led the prayers at Day's gravesite in his hometown of Warrnambool: 'Lord, hear the prayers we offer for John Day, your servant and priest. He faithfully fulfilled his ministry in Your name. May he rejoice forever in the fellowship of the saints.'

Never mind the fellowship. It was like they were burying a saint.

The report of Day's death was book-ended with an article by Father Pell, now Archbishop of Sydney, Cardinal George Pell, in which he ranted about the evils of television.

Melbourne's first Sunday newspaper, the *Melbourne Observer*, was less complimentary. On 13 August 1972, the paper ran with a screaming front page headline: 'RC Priest in Government Scandal.' Without mentioning any names, the article provided a very comprehensive account of what had taken place in Mildura. The story of Day getting pulled up in St Kilda in 1956 also got a run. The allegations made in the twelve statements I had obtained were dealt with in detail. My fate—the forced transfer that led to my resignation—was also addressed.

No doubt some at Russell Street would have assumed I was the source. I can see O'Connor looking at that headline and reading the report with gritted teeth. It wasn't me. It was a couple of detectives I knew from the armed robbery squad. I hadn't set them up for it, either. For some reason they had taken it upon themselves to get this story into the press. They contacted the *Melbourne Observer* and sold the story. My memory is that they received eighty dollars each. Hardly worth their efforts. Years later one of them paid me a visit and apologised for selling the story. I told them I didn't care what they had done.

Les Shilton continued to call for a judicial inquiry, but that horse had bolted. The Hamer government was re-elected with an increased majority in 1973, picking up four seats, one of them Shilton's.

Within a few days of leaving the force, I received a phone call from a very good friend, Sid Baker, who was the detective senior sergeant in charge of the CIB at Prahran, making the first of a number of impromptu job offers.

Sid told me he was disgusted by what had happened to me, and that a position would be made available for me at Prahran without me losing seniority or rank.

'You can do whatever you like,' Sid said. 'Until the day you retire.'

'Come on, Sid,' I told him. 'Stop bullshitting me. Jacko's put you up to this.'

At the time Jacko—Reg Jackson—was the chief commissioner of the Victoria Police force and a very good friend of Sid's.

Sid hesitated. 'Yes, he has, Dinny. Yeah.'

I knocked it back.

Harry McMenamin, a retired detective chief inspector and deputy head of the CIB, offered me a job working security at Georges, the exclusive department store in Melbourne. He didn't make the offer out of a sense of compassion or generosity; he made it to get me out of the road.

I could have taken these cushy jobs but I knew the offers were made only in an attempt to keep me quiet and get me out of Mildura, where any ongoing inquiry into Day would have lapsed into the void. I was a thorn in the side of the Catholic Church and the Victoria Police force.

Later in the year, I received another job offer from the Victorian chief stipendiary magistrate, Alf Foley. I knew Alf well, and had had a few beers with him over the years. He was a staunch, rock solid Catholic who was well regarded in the force.

Alf said, 'Dinny, this is Alf Foley. John MacArdle and I are going fishing up on the Darling and we need you as a guide.'

It was a strange request. I was shocked hearing his voice out of the blue. I hadn't heard from him in over ten years.

'Don't bullshit me, Alf. What's this all about?'

'Look, I tell you what. There's a position being created as head of the security group for the County Court, the Supreme Court and Petty Sessions. And you're the man for the job. What do you think?'

'First off, Alf, I don't want to go fishing. Second, I don't want the job.'

I had been through the wringer. I'd been forced out of my job because of my pursuit of Day. I was on the verge of a breakdown, and after I put the phone down, I burst into tears.

❖

Jean had always wanted to be a policeman's wife, so she became quite unhappy after I was forced to resign. She found herself more isolated than I was when I left the force, and it had a terrible effect on her. Her personality changed. She went from being a happy, fun-loving person to being withdrawn, almost lost. I've no doubt that my investigation into Day had stirred up some deeply repressed memories of her childhood.

She'd never been anything more than a light social drinker, but with her demons disturbed by the events in Mildura, she began to hit the bottle. She did it in a clandestine way, hiding the booze all over the house.

I tried to talk to her but she was retreating before my eyes. I suggested counselling but she wouldn't have a bar of it. Jean began a long descent into alcoholism and anguish from which she would never return. One day she said she was going down to Melbourne to find work. I didn't stop her; we needed the money. In 1980 she jumped on the train at Mildura, and she didn't come back.

I only saw Jean once more and that was three weeks later when I went down to sign the divorce papers. It saddened me, but there was nothing I could do. I think she had just had enough of Mildura. She was a city girl and that's where she wanted to be. My determination to bring Day to justice had driven her into her own personal hell. The whole business had affected her deeply and I felt that I was to blame. It had unlocked many unhappy memories of her childhood and the abuse she had suffered at the hands of her guardian.

After the divorce, she'd occasionally ring on some pretext or other but would want to talk about Day. Sometimes she posted me newspaper clippings about him. I'd also hear a whisper from Melbourne from time to time; she was hitting the drink harder and harder. It ended up taking her life in 2000.

My sons—Michael, Martin, Gavin and Anthony—have grown up to become fine young men. They know they owe their existence to their mother, Jean.

❖

After I left the force, I began to take an interest in local government. I'd always been keen on politics. The stuffing had been knocked out of me, and local politics and serving the community in Mildura was a means of alleviating my pain. I needed the involvement; it forced me to concentrate on other things. I ran for the Mildura Shire Council in October 1972 and was lucky enough to get the votes. I went on to become shire president of Mildura in 1979.

In 1980, I met up with Premier Hamer in my capacity as shire president. I was driving him around Mildura Shire, showing him some of the improvements the council had made. We were discussing state funding and money that had been made available by his government in the local area.

There was a pause in the conversation before Hamer said to me: 'Denis, if you were still a detective and the same situation arose as it did back then, would you do the same thing?'

I was astonished. The question had come like a bolt out of the blue. I took my time answering him.

'Yes, I would, Mr Premier,' I replied. 'But I do think the penalty was a bit harsh.'

He took his time to answer.

'Yes, it was.'

9

BLOODIED BUT UNBOWED

Blessed are those who are persecuted for the sake of righteousness: for theirs is the kingdom of heaven.
MATTHEW 5:10

I refer to your letter dated 16th August 2006 to Minister Holding regarding former Detective Senior Sergeant Constable Denis Ryan. This matter was referred to me by the Minister for consideration on 4th September 2006.

Since your letter, I have arranged for a comprehensive sworn statement to be taken from former Assistant Commissioner, Services Department, John O'Connor who worked as the Chief Commissioner's Special Investigator in 1972. At that time, Mr O'Connor was tasked by the Chief Commissioner, along with Detective Inspector Harvey Childs [sic] to personally investigate the reported misconduct by Monsignor John Day, parish priest at the Sacred Heart Church, Mildura.

This matter was subject to inquiries by the Mildura CIB at the time and Assistant Commissioner O'Connor met with Senior Constable Ryan and Detective Sergeant James Barritt in Mildura on 20 January 1972. Later that day, Assistant Commissioner O'Connor and

Detective Inspector Child interviewed nine youths, none of which made any allegations against Day.

Subsequently, Senior Constable Ryan did not produce any statement of complaint to Assistant Commissioner O'Connor however one statement alleging sexual assault by Monsignor Day was subsequently recorded.

Following extensive interviews and investigation the brief of evidence was referred to the Crown Solicitor's Office for approval to prosecute. The Crown Prosecutor did not approve the brief due to the lack of corroboration as was then legally required.

On 7th September 1972, Assistant Commissioner O'Connor met Denis Ryan again at the Mildura Court where unrelated charges against Detective Sergeant Barritt were heard and dismissed. Assistant Commissioner O'Connor inquired as to why Ryan had resigned from Victoria Police and he advised that it was because he could not get on with Sergeant Barritt.

Following examination of this extensive statement by former Assistant Commissioner O'Connor, I am completely satisfied with the conduct of the investigation into the Day matter and that Denis Ryan resigned from Victoria Police of his own accord.

I also attach for your records a copy of earlier advice to you dated 7th April 1998 from former deputy Commissioner O'Loughlin regarding the Ryan matter.

❖

The undated letter received by Russell Savage's office in September 2006 was signed by the then Chief Commissioner of the Victoria Police force, Ms Christine Nixon. The letter stands as the final official hurrah in this whole ugly episode.

Russell Savage was an independent member of the Victorian parliament's lower house seat of Mildura. He was elected in 1996 and held the seat for ten years. After the 1999 state election, he and two other independent MPs held the balance of power. The three agreed to support Labor and endorsed Steve Bracks as premier.

Born in Victoria, Savage had spent three years as a police officer in London's Metropolitan Police. He returned home and joined the Victoria Police force in 1970. He became a senior sergeant, and was stationed at Mildura in the 1970s and '80s.

Not long after he was elected to parliament, I spoke with Russell in his office. I told him the whole story—about the Day investigation, Barritt, and Irwin and O'Connor's cover up. About a year later, Russell contacted me and said he would like to help out in some way or another. He started stirring the pot.

On 6 August 2006, Russell Savage got to his feet in the Victorian Legislative Assembly and spoke of the miscarriages of justice suffered by Day's victims, and me, too, as the man who dedicated himself to bringing Day to justice. Russell requested the then police minister, Tim Holding, to instruct the police to hold an inquiry into the cover up.

Christine Nixon replied to Holding's request in a letter sent directly to Russell Savage. Never mind that she got my rank wrong in that shambolic letter, referring to me as Detective Senior Sergeant Constable Denis Ryan—a rank that doesn't exist—or that she misspelt Harvey Child's name.

Nixon relied solely on a sworn statement from Assistant Commissioner 'Baton Jack' O'Connor. She states that he interviewed nine of the twelve victims from whom I had taken statements in the course of my investigation into Day. That was the full extent of the inquiry as far as I can make out. Nixon sought and obtained a sworn statement from O'Connor: by the date of Nixon's letter he was an 89-year-old man who had retired from the police force twenty-four years before.

I have not seen O'Connor's statement. I don't know if it was the one he made in 1972 when he put the smother on, or if he was called out of retirement to provide his recollections. The statement to which Nixon refers was not made publicly available. What I can say is that I spoke to seven of the victims after Savage passed this letter on to me, and after my inquiries only one had been interviewed by O'Connor and his sidekick, Harvey Child. That was in Melbourne in 1972. This victim confirmed he had been interviewed by O'Connor and Child and told me he had confirmed the allegations he had made in his original statement almost word for word.

The other six had not been approached at all, but when I spoke to them, they all stood by their allegations of sexual abuse at the hands of Day.

The victims I had been unable to contact had either left the Mildura area or moved on to another plane. I knew some had met a grisly fate.

O'Connor had eaten at my house. We had got drunk as louts together. I came to learn that he was an ardent and bigoted Catholic—a man of deeply embedded prejudices. Nixon's letter indicates that, thirty-four years later, the Victoria Police force continued to believe the lie of O'Connor's investigation.

When he put the smother on, O'Connor was a chief superintendent. He failed to live up to his boast made to me one drunken afternoon many years ago that he would make chief commissioner. But 'Baton Jack' O'Connor got close. O'Connor retired from the force as an assistant commissioner.

My guess is that Christine Nixon—the first woman police commissioner in Australia—was mushroomed by O'Connor: kept in the dark and fed bullshit. And O'Connor was a master bullshit artist.

❖

In 2006 I received another letter from Russell Savage. Russell attached a letter from Bill Hager, a retired police officer who had been stationed at Edenhope, in the Wimmera near the South Australian border, in the mid-1970s. Hager wrote that in the early hours of New Year's Day 1976, he had pulled over a local priest. Hager wrote that when the priest refused a breath test, he was arrested and taken into custody. Hager and a Constable Schulz prepared a brief of evidence for divisional headquarters in Hamilton and sent it to the attention of an inspector there. The brief got to Superintendent Pat Cashin, an ardent Catholic and a former inspector at Mildura during my time there. Cashin jumped on the drink-drive charge, but Hager was not prepared to let it go.

Hager was put through the wringer, just as I had been. He was marched into Chief Commissioner Jackson's office where Jackson and the then Deputy Commissioner Ron Braybrook, his judge and jury, threatened him with a transfer if he persisted in charging the priest. But Hager remained adamant that he would not drop the charges.

Ultimately Hager was shanghaied out of Edenhope. He ended up taking a posting at Nagambie in central Victoria for his 'own peace of mind'. The priest was never prosecuted. Hager learnt through the grapevine that, due to his heavy drinking, the priest was continually transferred from parish to parish within the Ballarat diocese.

Hager's letter described a running joke among police officers in the Hamilton district at the time that Cashin 'had an extraneous appointment to the Bishop to protect priests from prosecution'. The Catholic Mafia was alive and bringing influence to bear in 1976.

❖

There have been changes, most for the good, and I expect the bad old days of sectarianism in the force are long past, and not before time.

The Roman Catholic Church has been forced to confront its demons. Apologies have been made. The then pope, Pope Benedict XVI, apologised. All the Church's senior clerics, archbishops and bishops have offered apologies of one type or another. But what are they apologising for?

The apologies take the form of expressions of sorrow and regret for aberrant priests disgracing themselves and causing hurt and pain among parishioners. What is not acknowledged is that the Church has covered up the crimes of priests like Day. The cover up simply increased the offending, because Day and his ilk understood that they could rape children and never have to face the consequences. The effect of the cover up was to create an epidemic of paedophilia in Australia, and its epicentre was the Ballarat diocese.

Nowhere in Australia, and as far as I can determine nowhere on earth, has this epidemic of paedophilia been as pronounced or as gravely damaging as it was in the Ballarat diocese. There is not a country town in western Victoria that has not been affected by it. Towns like Colac, Horsham, Stawell, Ararat, Apollo Bay, Mildura and Ballarat itself now bear the scars, the pain and the trauma of decades of abuse perpetrated by paedophile priests.

The epidemic of paedophilia was driven by paedophile priests, and the worst of them all was Monsignor John Day, who died unrepentant and unpunished. Convicted paedophile priest Gerald Ridsdale has acknowledged that his victims number in the hundreds. Ridsdale was convicted of rape, buggery and indecent assault of boys in Bacchus Marsh, Ballarat, Warrnambool, Edenhope, Horsham and Mortlake over two decades.

By my reckoning, Day was much worse. He had been an active paedophile within the same diocese for forty-eight years, committing his crimes against children without let or hindrance. And in Mildura, Day was protected and cosseted by Barritt, a corrupt police detective, and Kearney, a supplicant with a vicious criminal streak. Day's power in this community was almost absolute. He wielded the power of life and death in Mildura for thirteen years.

Many of his victims cannot come forward. Some have committed suicide—at least seven by my count—others have descended into alcoholism and drug abuse. Some remain so deeply traumatised that they are unable to acknowledge the crimes perpetrated upon them. These young lives were rent asunder; their emotional development was halted, their love of school and education abruptly curtailed.

Today, the Sacred Heart Church in Mildura looks more like a cathedral than a parish church, and its vastness is due almost entirely to Monsignor Day's extortion of money from local people.

Day's name appears in a publication to commemorate the centenary of the Catholic Church in Mildura. He is praised for his work in extending the old church into its present glory and purchasing land around it. In the penultimate paragraph, the only acknowledgment of Day's depravity appears as a laughable euphemism: 'Later extreme hurt, pain and disappointment caused by some aspects of Father Day's life surfaced amongst Mildura parishioners.'

What has not been acknowledged is that the Church has covered up the crimes of paedophile priests like Day and Ridsdale and, in doing so, increased exponentially the number of victims and offences against them.

The Roman Catholic Church in Australia has installed its Towards Healing process. It is an opportunity for victims to be compensated and for apologies to be made. No doubt the money has been welcomed by some, but all of Day's victims would acknowledge that money on its own cannot properly resolve the sins of the past.

All of the victims I have spoken to have been left deeply dissatisfied with Towards Healing. Compensation bought silence. If a victim took the cheque, they had to sign a non-disclosure guarantee. This meant their experiences would continue as dirty secrets. For some the money only plunged them further into darkness—alcoholism, drug and gambling addictions.

In the United States the cost of litigation has bankrupted entire dioceses, with the cost of each victim's claim averaging $1 million. In Australia, the Towards Healing process has cost the Church a good deal less. I have spoken to a number of victims. Their payments have varied but they seem infinitesimal compared to the suffering they have endured: $25,000 here, $40,000 there. Sometimes more. Sometimes less.

Certainly by US standards, the compensation figures are miserable amounts.

Sometimes the money has been more of a curse than a blessing. Many victims have been deeply traumatised by Day's abuse and have lived lives of financial and intellectual poverty. Placing a relatively large amount of money in their hands has not always been in the best interests of their health and welfare. Some successful claimants have withdrawn into alcoholic or narcotic fogs until the money runs out, only to emerge with minds even more troubled. Others have engaged in almighty and pointless binges, never to emerge.

Peter Connors was installed as Bishop of the Ballarat diocese in 1997, ending Mulkearns's twenty-six years as bishop of Ballarat. In 2006, Bishop Connors asked if he could come and see me. I wasn't thrilled at the prospect but I agreed. He drove up to my home in Red Cliffs in one of the diocesan cars. Unlike his predecessor, Bishop Connors did not demand that I kiss his episcopal ring. Instead he extended his hand. I shook it and looked him in the eye.

'Call me Peter,' he said. I gather the main purpose of his visit was to tell me the bad news that I was not eligible for compensation under Towards Healing. I was not a victim as such, he explained. I nodded.

'So what can you tell me about Day?' I asked.

'I believe he was a serious offender,' Connors replied.

'Have you had many applying for compensation through Towards Healing as a result of Day?'

'Yes.'

'Would there be a hundred?'

'Yes.'

'In Mildura?'

'Yes.'

'More than a hundred?'

'Yes.'

'Did many of the victims suffer buggery?'

'Yes.'

'The others were sexual assaults and acts of gross indecency?'

'Yes.'

I didn't want the question and answer to continue. I had heard enough. I told him to leave. I wasn't rude but I was brusque. I thanked Connors for visiting me and for being honest. We shook hands and he left.

I regret being abrupt with him now. Bishop Connors at least did his best to deal with the matters that had been left to him—the weeping sores of the Ballarat diocese.

Apologies and guilt money will only take people so far. Those who covered up for these criminal priests need to be brought to book. Though many have passed on, others remain who have said nothing and have done nothing that would add to our knowledge and thus our understanding of how this behaviour was allowed to occur.

Just as thousands of child sex offences have been committed, a substantial body of evidence also exists to indicate the concealing of crimes or persuading people not to give evidence about a crime, conspiracies, perversion of the course of justice, and of priests and bishops being accessories before and after the fact. The men who committed these crimes, some of them senior clerics, need to feel the full force of the law. And those who have shuffled off this mortal coil should not be spared their share of opprobrium just because they're not here to listen to it.

❖

In 2012, when the Victoria Police force put its submission to the Victorian parliamentary inquiry into child abuse by religious and other organisations, describing it as exhaustively researched over more than sixty years, it laid the overwhelming share of the blame at the feet of the Roman Catholic Church. The submission indicated that the Church had never referred any complaint directly to the police and that it had been unco-operative with police.

When Deputy Commissioner Graham Ashton gave evidence at the parliamentary inquiry on 19 October 2012, he rounded on the Catholic Church and its failure to assist police: 'Examples of the historic activities include transferring alleged offenders to other parishes or schools within Victoria, interstate or overseas, permitting international trips to undergo spiritual formation amidst child sexual abuse allegations.'

It might be that, when it comes to investigating Catholic priests, the Victoria Police force is *now* squeaky clean. I wouldn't know. I've been out of the job too long. But it was going on when I was a copper and it was still going on after I left.

It is sometimes said that one of the primary reasons for the existence of paedophile priests is the vow of chastity that a priest takes, resulting in an overt act of sexual repression that bubbles away in the human libido, only to find expression in paedophilia. The theory goes that if you take away the vow of chastity, the problem will largely be solved. This is a gross oversimplification. Had priests engaged in consensual sex with other adults, we would not be so concerned, and they would have committed no crime under the law of the land.

The reality is that a paedophile priest like Day committed crimes against children because he could. Day held power over children and understood that he could commit acts of gross indecency, sexual assault, buggery and rape on children with impunity. Kids feared him. Day's victims were threatened and bullied into trembling, silent compliance.

The Roman Catholic Church's response to this sad episode in Australian history was invariably directed at avoiding damage to its reputation. The unwillingness or the inability of the Church to confront its paedophile priests and assist in bringing them before the courts has been the major contributing factor to this epidemic of paedophilia in post-war Australia.

AFTERWORD

A royal commission is a broody hen sitting on a china egg.
MICHAEL FOOT, 1913–2010

Now we have a royal commission. I welcome it. When it was announced in November 2012, I jumped for joy.

I am glad that the commission will not just investigate the Catholic Church but all organisations, religious or otherwise, and investigate the criminal sexual abuse of children and why they systematically failed to respond. The Roman Catholic Church does not have a monopoly on this appalling conduct but it is clear that it has been the principal perpetrator.

The commissioners face enormous challenges. The scale of institutional child sex abuse in this country is virtually without precedent anywhere in the world. The commissioners' primary objective will be to learn as much as they can from victims and to direct governments, both state and federal, to create systems that will not fail children.

The victims of paedophiles like Monsignor John Day should have the opportunity to tell their stories to the commission. There are thousands of victims and their voices must be heard. But the victims need more. They need to see the wheels of justice turn in the right direction. Where possible, the victims need to see their tormentors in the dock.

The commission should investigate how an organisation like the Roman Catholic Church can allow its own laws to override the laws of the land and why, when the Church sees conflict between canon law and Australian law, canon law is assumed to take precedence.

Most importantly, a royal commission should examine the effectiveness of police in investigating allegations of institutional child sex abuse. There is too much evidence indicating that elements of the police across Australia have failed to investigate these matters properly. My story might fall into the category of the worst example of police collusion with child sex offenders. In 1958 I locked up a Methodist minister who got thirteen years for raping and abusing boys in his care. Yet it was another twenty years before the first Catholic priest was convicted of child sex offences in Victoria, and another fifteen before Ridsdale became the second Catholic priest to find his way into the courts for sex offences against children.

The obstructionism of the Church goes only part of the way to explaining why there were no convictions recorded against Catholic priests for child sex offending when clearly there was so much offending going on. I can attest to the fact that an element within the Victoria Police force existed between the 1950s and 1970s and that its primary purpose was to ensure that Catholic priests who committed offences did not have their days in court. I was asked to join it. I was told that this group took its instructions 'from the Cathedral'. I can also confirm this group's ruthless efficiency in achieving its aims. I am living proof of it. It has become the story of my life.

I have battled with the demons every day for the past forty years. I have made mistakes in my life—plenty since I left the force and plenty while I was in it—but I maintain that when I was called upon to do my duty, I did it. I can't say the same for many of my senior officers.

Day, Barritt, Kearney, the Catholic Mafia—I look back on it as a nightmare now. And it's a nightmare that never ends. I still wake up in a cold sweat almost every night. It was all over bar the shouting forty years ago but the images of Day molesting children, Barritt standing over a parent or Kearney raping that poor young woman continue to haunt my dreams.

No doubt the royal commission will see a flood of apologies from any number of government and non-government organisations who have failed in their duty of care to children. It's the first step in the process. It shouldn't be the only one.

If apologies are going to be made, one to me from the Victoria Police force might be nice, too. But I won't be holding my breath.

I'm Dinny Ryan and I have just turned 81 years of age.

DAY AND THE DARKNESS: THREE VICTIMS SPEAK

John's story

John Fitzgibbon was 10 years old and in grade 6 at Sacred Heart Primary School when he was first raped by John Day in 1958. The sexual abuse continued for two years. Day referred to John as his 'favourite', and threatened him with being sent to a boys' home if the boy told anyone about the abuse. John had been a good student at school and had received good reports in grade five, but once the abuse commenced, he lost all desire for education and feared school, as this was the place where Day abused him.

John has lived in Mildura all his life. With the encouragement of his friend Judy, whom he used to meet around the riverbank in Mildura when he skipped school, he began to write to ease the pain of his abuse. He filled exercise books with his thoughts and experiences.

Forty years later, he discovered the exercise books and began chronicling the pain he suffered at the hands of Day in a manuscript. Entitled Misspent Youth, *this is a powerful and moving portrayal of John's life and his lifelong struggle to overcome the trauma he encountered as a 10-year-old boy.*

The following is an edited extract from John's manuscript, detailing his first encounters with Day.

Two grades went that day: about 160 kids walked over to the church for confession. As usual the nuns organised the kids to each confession box so the numbers were even.

As I was walking down the aisle, Sister Claude stopped me and made me sit alongside her near the aisle.

Sister Claude gave me a poke with her leather strap and nodded in the direction of one of the four confession boxes. At first I couldn't see but my eyes quickly grew used to the light. I could see a shadow through the partition, like a silhouette, and when the figure spoke, I could tell it was Father Day.

Unlike the other priests, he took a long time and kept asking me if there was anything else I should tell him. I didn't have anything to confess but he persisted and urged me to tell him all of my sins.

All I could say was, 'Bless me, Father for I have sinned', but he didn't seem to think that was enough.

Finally he let me go, telling me to say so many Hail Marys. I made a point of trying to avoid him at confession in future.

Later that afternoon in the church, Father Day gave a sermon. He went on and on about the fires of hell and told us that, as children, we must keep our souls pure through communion.

As we lined up to take communion, the altar boys were kept busy handing the sacramental bread to Father Day. As my turn came, Father Day put his hand on my head. He hadn't done that with any of the other kids.

I kept thinking that he thought I might have lied to him in the confessional box and that he had special powers that could see into my soul and tell him everything that I had been up to.

The following day, I got into a bit of strife in Sister Claude's class. She was a bully and a sadist, and everyone was frightened of her. We had seen her use the strap on kids, and others had their faces slapped so hard they would just burst into tears.

But kids were still kids and when she had her back turned, the boy sitting next to me and I started hitting each other on the legs. As I gave the boy a hard slap on his thigh, Sister Claude swung around and turned towards me.

'Mr Fitzgibbon, you come up here now.'

It was nearly lunchtime and I didn't think too much would happen. Maybe I'd have to stay in class over lunch but I figured she'd want her lunch break so I would probably avoid that leather strap she carried with her all the time.

I wasn't so lucky. As the bell went and the kids filed out of the room, Sister grabbed me by the arm and dragged me out. My feet were barely touching the floor and my arm hurt from her tight grip.

She dragged me across the schoolyard and towards the presbytery. There were other kids pointing at me and somehow they knew that I was in deep trouble. Maybe most thought I was getting the strap but some of them would have known better.

I could see Father Day sitting on a chair on the verandah at the presbytery and he was looking at me as Sister dragged me towards him.

'Excuse me, Father, but this boy has been naughty and I would like you to deal with him,' she said, dragging me up the two steps to the verandah.

'Don't worry, Sister,' Day replied. 'I'll deal with him.'

I took the two steps up on to the presbytery verandah slowly, unsure of my fate. I stood some distance from Father Day with my head bowed.

'Well, what do you have to say for yourself, young man?' he asked sternly.

'I am sorry, Father,' I blurted out. I was nearly peeing myself by this stage.

'Make sure you say that at your next confession,' he told me. 'What will you say?'

'I'm sorry. I've been bad in class, Father.'

'Good boy. You don't want me to tell your parents, do you?'

'No, Father. Please, no.'

'OK. You run along now and I will be watching you from now on. I will speak with you again.'

'Yes, Father. Thank you, Father.'

As I walked back to the playground, I turned and looked at Father Day as he was going through the door of the presbytery. I walked past the peppercorn trees and remembered how the old nuns would use the branches as whips, belting us on the backs of our legs.

I couldn't see any of my classmates but I could hear them in the distance playing in the yard. I could even hear the football being kicked around.

I looked up into one of the trees and decided to clamber up it as high as I could go. From my vantage point I could see the kids playing football. I was wondering what I had done wrong and why I was the only one to be sent to see Father Day.

I sat up there looking around, feeling safe. The bell went to end lunch but I thought I'd stay up in that old tree. I might get in trouble for being late but then Sister Claude wouldn't know how long I'd spent with Father Day, so I thought I'd be all right.

I must have stayed in that tree for another hour before I climbed down and went back to class.

Sure enough, when I got back Sister Claude didn't say a thing.

At afternoon play time, some of the kids asked me what had happened with Father Day. There was nothing to tell. All I told them was what he had said, that he'd be watching me.

A week later, the grade sixers were headed off for confession and mass again.

All week I'd been thinking about it. I wanted to avoid doing confession with Father Day.

Again Sister Claude was fussing around us, making sure the numbers were even around the confessional. I saw the four priests walk in, including Father Day. As he was about to get into his box, he turned and smiled at me.

I was desperate to avoid him but when my time came, Sister Claude nudged me with her strap in her hand and pointed towards Father Day's confessional.

'Bless me, Father, for I have sinned,' I blurted out. 'It has been five days since my last confession.'

I paused to hear his response. The confession box seemed darker than usual.

'Yes, my son,' Father Day replied finally. 'What are your sins?'

'I was bad in school, Father.'

'What did you do?'

'I was messing around with another boy and I whacked him. Just messing around, Father.'

'Hitting someone is not messing around, my son. So what other sins are on your soul?'

'I swore in the school grounds, Father.'

'You are at a Catholic school. We do not stand for that sort of thing. You know that, don't you?

'Yes, Father.'

'Any other sins on your soul, my boy?'

'No, Father.'

'Your sins are serious, my son. I would like to see you soon about these, especially you hitting the boy in your class.'

'Yes, Father.'

'Your penance for your sins will be six Our Fathers and six Hail Marys.'

Father Day then said something in Latin while I waited.

'You may go now, my son.'

As I walked out of the box, Sister Claude was giving me a glare as if I had done something wrong. I couldn't work out why I was in such trouble just for messing around in class. I just wanted it to be over.

I knelt down and started to say my penance. I could feel Sister Claude's eyes on me. Most of the other kids had finished their penance. There were only a few others left. Sister Claude moved down the aisle.

I thought, here's my chance to escape, knowing that her

veil was like blinkers on a horse. I moved quietly down the aisle, heading towards the exit. I was almost out the door when I felt Sister Claude's sharp grip on my arm. She pulled me back to my seat and as I sat there two girls sniggered at me behind their hands.

I stayed there under Sister Claude's fierce gaze while all the children filed out of the church, leaving me, her and the priests in the church.

Then I saw Father Day emerge from his box and come straight over.

'Yes, young Johnny, isn't it?'

I didn't have a chance to say anything. Sister Claude chipped in.

'Yes, Father. That's him,' she said.

'Thank you, Sister. Now come with me, young man. You have a few lessons to learn about behaviour at school. Come now. I won't bite.'

Father Day placed his hand in the small of my back and led me away through the front of the church and towards the presbytery.

'Would you like a lemonade, Johnny?' Father Day asked. His stern demeanour had slipped. He seemed friendly but in a way it was even more scary.

'No, thank you, Father,' I replied. A drink was the last thing I needed. I was busting to go to the toilet and being with Father Day in the presbytery had made it even worse.

'Yes, you do, Johnny,' Father Day said with that stern tone back in his voice. 'You have a drink and we'll have a talk, OK?'

He led me into a darkened room and went out to the kitchen to get me a drink. The room had a couch alongside one wall and a little table sat in the middle of the room with a number of books stacked up on it. On the other side of the room there were two armchairs side by side. Above the chairs there was a painting of the Last Supper.

Now I really wanted to pee and I started crossing my legs to ease the pressure on my bladder.

Father Day walked back in with a glass of lemonade in his hand. He pushed the books on the table to one side and put the glass down.

'Here's your drink, young man. Come over here and sit down,' he said, nodding at one of the armchairs.

'May I please use the toilet, Father?'

'Well now, yes you could, but there's a meeting in the next room. We can't have you disturbing the meeting, walking through to the toilet,' he said with a look of amusement on his face. 'I tell you what, I'll get a bucket for you. You can pee in that. It's just outside. I'll get it for you.'

The fear and my full bladder had other ideas. I was already wetting my pants, little dribbles coming out that I couldn't stop, no matter how hard I tried.

Day came back in, brandishing an old metal bucket.

'Here we are,' he said. 'Use this.'

I looked from side to side. I didn't want to go to the toilet in front of a priest.

'You and I have the same equipment. Would you like me to help you?' Father Day said, still holding the bucket.

'I'm OK. Thank you, Father.'

I took the bucket from his hand and put it on the floor. I

turned around, my back facing Father Day for some privacy. As I fumbled with my fly, I started peeing myself. I weed into the bucket but most of it sprayed on my pants.

'My, you did want to go, didn't you, Johnny?' Father Day said, smiling even more broadly. 'I'll get a towel and we will clean you up in no time. There's a towel right here on the couch. Take your pants off and they will be dry in no time.'

'It's OK, Father,' I stammered out, confused and in a panic. 'By the time I get back to school, I'll be dry.'

'We haven't had our talk yet, Johnny. So get those pants off and sit down.'

I didn't get a chance to undress. Father Day came over and pulled my pants down. He pushed me towards the couch and I sat down as he pulled my pants off over my shoes and socks.

Then he grabbed at my underpants. I squirmed and grabbed at the band and pulled them back up.

'It's OK,' Father Day said. 'Let go now. You can't have wet undies on.'

He pulled my underpants down and slid them off. I sat there covering myself with my shirt while he fussed around hanging up my pants and undies.

'Now that wasn't so bad, was it, son?' Father Day said as he sat alongside me. 'We can have our talk now.'

'Yes, Father.'

'That's my boy,' he said as he slipped his arm around me. 'Now let's talk about you hitting boys in class. That is very serious, Johnny. Do you want me to tell your parents?'

'No, please, Father.'

'I think I should.'

'No, Father. No.'

He started wiping my legs with the towel, moving up to my private parts then back down my legs.

'Now that feels good, doesn't it,' he said. 'Just relax. I won't hurt you and I won't tell your parents if you're a good boy. Just lay back. Let your shirt go. It's OK.'

He kept rubbing me with the towel, getting close to my private parts again.

'You're a very special boy,' he said, looking at me. 'Now roll onto your side and I'll do the backs of your legs.'

He started wiping the towel over my bottom and between my legs. He clasped my penis with his hand. I felt a pain in my stomach and I was so frightened I couldn't speak.

'That feel good, Johnny?' he said. 'I've got one just like yours but it's bigger. Would you like to look at it and see?'

He grabbed my hand and rolled me back over. I could see he had his pants down. His penis was hard and sticking out. I didn't understand what was going on.

'Give me your hand and hold it like this,' he said as he took my hand firmly. I wanted to resist but he was too strong. He guided my hand towards his penis and made me hold it and move it back and forth.

'Yours will be big just like mine one day when you're older and it will get hard like mine,' he said, moving my hand up and down his penis. 'Now this is our secret, OK?'

I couldn't say anything. I wanted to cry but I wasn't game. The pain in my stomach grew sharper. My throat was dry.

He rolled me over again on to my stomach and put his knees on each side of me. I felt his penis between the cheeks of my bum, going back and forth. He gasped and then I felt something warm and wet on the backs of my legs. I thought he might have peed himself. But this wasn't pee.

I lay there for what seemed like hours before he got up off me.

'You're special, Johnny,' Father Day said, standing in front of me while I lay on my belly. 'This is our secret, OK? You tell anyone and I'll tell your parents that you've been bad at school. They won't believe anything you tell them anyway.'

I didn't understand what had just happened and I didn't know what the warm liquid he'd squirted on me was. He started to wipe the cheeks of my bum with the towel again.

'Now, my son, get dressed. Your pants and undies should be dry by now,' he told me. 'Get dressed and I'll get something special for you.'

He walked out of the room. I scrambled for my pants. I couldn't get dressed quick enough.

Within seconds, he was back in the room again.

'That was quick,' he said. 'Here are some lovely chocolates for you.'

He handed me the chocolates.

'Special chocolates for a special boy.'

'Yes, Father.'

'Run along and get back to school. Be a good boy. And don't forget, this is our little secret.'

'Yes, Father.'

I took off as fast as I could back to class but as I ran past the old peppercorn trees, I stopped and climbed up the big one again, going as high as I could. I sat there in the branches of that tree for an hour or more, crying. I didn't understand what had happened but I felt an intense feeling of shame and fear.

I just knew I didn't want it to happen again.

Kym's story

In 1957, when he was 11 years old, Kym Burford was raped by John Day on four occasions. On each occasion Kym was in the company of Day for a weekend trip to Melbourne. Kym was raped at Day's sister's home in Williamstown. The tiny cottage had just one spare bedroom with one double bed. Day would demand that Kym sleep with him in that bed.

The memories never leave you. At a subconscious level, they're always alive and lurching around in the dark corners of my mind. I never quite understand why they spring forward into the here and now when they do. I might be hosing the garden or messing around in the shed, loading up the ute or driving down the road. There's no accounting for it and no telling when it will happen.

When the memories come, his face will loom up at me, just like it had back when I was a kid. Or I'd be back sitting on the bench seat of his big car, the bastard asking me to grab the wheel while he undid his fly and that bloody ugly dog of his grinned stupidly at us from the back seat.

I live on the pension, having retired a few years ago. I'd been a plumber all my working life. I still keep myself busy, pottering around, fixing things that need some attention.

I've been married for forty-four years. We have three boys. They all followed the old man's trade. They're all plumbers and doing well for themselves.

I was born in Warrnambool and spent the first few years of my life there. My dad ran a trucking company, carting stock between Mt Gambier and Melbourne. He was doing all right for himself, too. We lived in a big house in Warrnambool, right behind Fletcher Jones. When my dad and mum split, my sister and I took off with Dad and moved up to Mildura. I would have been 8 or 9 at the time. My sister was a year younger.

We stayed with my two aunts, Phyllis and Gwen, who ran a guesthouse in Heron Avenue. I'd never met them before Dad and Mum split up. Old Phyllis and Gwen were devout Catholics, and the walls of the guesthouse were plastered with religious paintings and crucifixes. Phyllis and Gwen would go to mass almost every day, and sometimes twice on Sundays.

It was a bit confusing at first. We hadn't been a religious family but with Dad away a lot of the time, finding work wherever he could, I got stuck into it through my aunties.

I went to Sacred Heart Primary School in Mildura. I must have started off there in grade five. A few years back I went back to the school to ask for my student records but they clammed up and wouldn't give them to me.

Back then I loved school. I was into everything at Sacred Heart when I first got there—school plays, sport. I loved the place and loved the kids in my class. We were all pretty close. Big classrooms in those day—fifty or sixty kids in a class. The classrooms were bulging at the seams but we all got on pretty well. There weren't any blues, or nothing more than you might get anywhere else. Everyone just got stuck in and did the best they could.

Every now and then, we'd see Father Day walk around the playground. Everyone was a bit scared of him. He was the boss, the only adult male at the school. The rest of the teachers were nuns.

I got good reports. I was going pretty well. I enjoyed being there.

When I got to grade six, Sister Mary-Bernadette asked for volunteers to be altar boys. My hand shot straight up in the air. I wasn't the only one. There would have been fifteen or so boys who wanted to be in it. Sister took our names down and sent them over to Father Day in the presbytery. I'd volunteered because I wanted my aunts to be proud of me; Dad, too, but I didn't think I stood a chance. I was good at school but I was still a new kid in the town.

When the news came through I was almost as excited as my aunties. I was an altar boy. They stood around me and crowed. Becoming an altar boy was like Phyllis and Gwen making a name for themselves in the parish. They were as proud as punch.

Looking back I realise the game that Day was playing. Here I was from a broken home. My two aunties were my guardians. You wouldn't find more devoted, manic Catholics in the Vatican than Phyllis and Gwen. Day had taken all that into account. He'd done the calculations in that seedy, dark mind of his. Even if I'd spoken up and told my aunties what he'd done to me, I wouldn't have been believed. I was the perfect target.

But I didn't speak up. It took me ten years before I spoke to anyone about it, and only then when Dinny Ryan called me into the cop shop for a chat.

I was always the first into the church, getting the communion wine and wafers out, lighting the candles. The masses mid-week were sparsely attended. Sometimes, I'd look down and see only two men, sitting up the back of the church: Jim Barritt and Joe Kearney, dressed up like pox doctors' clerks.

It started when Day asked my aunties if I'd like to take a trip with him to Melbourne. 'Oh, yes, Father,' they'd gush excitedly. They were so proud that Father was taking such an interest in me.

At first I didn't know what was going to happen in Melbourne. By the second trip, I knew what to expect but I couldn't say no. My aunties would have been devastated. I couldn't tell anyone.

In the end there were four trips. I grew to dread them. Day would often take me to the pictures. There was a cinema in Bourke Street where the ceiling was painted with stars. When the lights went out, the stars would glisten and gleam on the ceiling. I'd look up and stare at them, almost willing the moment to freeze in time or at least delay the end of the movie for as long as possible.

Of course, it didn't happen. When the movie ended, we'd go to his sister's house in Williamstown. She'd have a meal ready for us to eat and as soon as the last scrap of food was off my plate, Day would make his excuses.

We were tired from the trip and would be going to bed early, he'd tell his sister. In that little bedroom, I'd scrunch my body up as far as I could against the wall but it was no use. I'd struggle as much as I could but I was just a scrawny kid. He was stronger than me.

Attempted buggery is what Dinny Ryan called it. I call it rape. Four times Day tried to stick his dick inside me. Each time it hurt and I wriggled and writhed so he couldn't go any further. In the end he grew tired of it. He'd get his dick inside me just a little bit and I'd yell out in pain. He'd pull back. Sometimes he'd masturbate. Other times he'd grab my penis and rub it.

Other times, I'd wake up with him holding me and kissing my head, and he'd try and put it in again.

I have no doubt his sister heard us. She must have known what was going on.

Sometimes during the drive he'd get his penis out and ask me to play with it. Once on a drive down to Melbourne, we were driving one of the nuns down to Ararat. Day made the seating arrangements. Sister would sit at the passenger door, and I'd be in the middle with Day at the wheel.

He had a rug spread over all our laps. And while he drove down to Ararat with Sister sitting next to me, he pulled his penis out and grabbed my hand and guided me towards his dick.

That was what Day was like: brazen, no fear, no consideration of the consequences. I often think some of the sisters knew about him and what he got up to. If they did, they never said boo. He had them under his thumb anyway.

By the end of the school year, I'd had enough. My reports were terrible that year. In that short time, I'd gone from a good student to a poor one. I didn't want to go to St Joseph's. I told my dad that. He got two jobs and was making enough money to give me and my sister the best education he could.

I was sent down to St Pat's in Ballarat as a boarder. I hated it from day one. I didn't suffer like I did with Day, but the brothers there were real bastards. After finishing first form, I told my dad I'd jump the fence if he sent me back.

'I'm not going back to no Catholic school,' I told him. He accepted that and I went to Mildura Tech. I got through it and started my apprenticeship.

And there I was doing my fourth year as an apprentice, doing a big job at the Murray Hotel.

Dinny Ryan walked in and told me he wanted me to come down to the police station for a word. I'd never met Dinny before that. I knew he was a copper, a detective, but I didn't know much about him. It was Barritt I was terrified of. I'd heard stories where he'd grab young blokes like me off the street and give them a flogging. He was king of the pricks. Bloody good Catholic though, sitting up the back of the church with his mate Kearney. I remember that.

I thought Dinny might have had me for speeding around town. I was pretty toey by the time I got to the police station.

He told me he was investigating Day for sex offences against children. I hadn't spoken to anyone about it since it happened. I thought, 'You bloody beauty! Justice at last for that bastard.'

As I started giving my statement to Dinny, I felt like I might not be able to stop. When it was done, I felt this enormous sense of relief, like a four-tonne boulder had been lifted off my shoulders.

'Am I the only one?' I asked.

'No,' Dinny told me. 'You are one of many and there will be many more.'

I really had thought I was the only one. Why had Day chosen me? It had driven me into a frenzy of guilt, doubt, anger and despair. Any relief I felt was short-lived.

I left the police station thinking Day was going to get arrested, hauled off in front of a judge and sent to jail, not just for what he did to me but for what he'd done to us all in Mildura.

I waited and waited but I didn't hear a word. Day was never charged. Later, I heard that Dinny had left the force. He'd come off second best, too. At the time, I didn't understand the forces that were at work and how powerful they were. It doesn't get any more formidable than the Catholic Church, and when I hear about how some of the coppers might have been involved in the cover up, it makes sense that what happened to me would be swept under the rug. I was just a tiny cog in a giant wheel.

A few years after I gave my statement to Dinny, I noticed an ad in the paper from a local lawyer, calling for anyone who'd been at Sacred Heart during the time I was there. I went in to the lawyer's office and she asked me a couple of questions. I didn't hear a peep about it for months until one day I got a letter in the mail.

The letter had a cheque in it for $7000. It was deemed full and final payment from the Roman Catholic Church. I thought, 'Crikey, is that all my life's worth?'

I was doing it tough at the time, so I snaffled the cheque.

In the end, it's not about money or compensation. How do you begin to come up with a number to compensate me for what Day had done to me? To this day, I still have trouble with my emotions. I'm a pretty laidback bloke but I often think that I don't feel things the way other people do. It might be the death of a pet or even a friend. Other people will open right up, but I just don't feel the same way. I worry that sometimes I don't feel anything.

And I run a mile from conflict. I can't stand it. I'll always be the one to try and smooth things over. Raised voices, anger. I just can't deal with them.

Like Popeye, I am what I am, but it's impossible to avoid the reality that the person I am was forged in the crucible of Day's abuse, like my emotional development stopped or was placed on hold when I was just 11 years of age.

I'm lucky to have had good people around me—my wife, my kids, good mates, too. I've been up front about this with them, told them everything there is. My wife had said I shouldn't waste time dredging up the past; that no good would come of it. She was only looking after me. But after I got talking to Dinny again a while back, she noticed it was doing me good to talk about it. She and the kids have supported me and that's a big help.

If the Catholic Church wanted to pay me a big cheque, I'm happy to say I'd take it, no questions asked. God knows, they've got more than me. But money is just a part of it. I'd like an apology. And not just the empty apologies that have been made in the past. Not just the 'We're sorry Monsignor John Day was a paedophile who abused you' type of apology but a real apology that acknowledged all of his crimes and the crimes of those who covered up for him. Those people in the Catholic Church who allowed Day to commit his crimes and by their nods and winks made it easier for him to continue raping and abusing children for forty years. The church needs to apologise for that. To date, they have only ummed and ahed their apologies.

They're not fair dinkum and they won't get the nod from me until they get fair dinkum.

Terry's story

Terry (not his real name) grew up in Apollo Bay in the 1950s. He was not a Catholic, and he attended the local state primary school. He was first raped by Day at 11 years of age. At the time, Day was established as the parish priest in Mildura but he regularly returned to his old parish of Apollo Bay to rape and molest a group of boys he referred to as his 'young friends'.

Over a three-year period Terry was raped by Day on as many as thirty occasions.

Terry could never bring himself to tell his parents about the sexual abuse he suffered at the hands of Day. To this day, he cannot tell his children.

Terry is now in his sixties. He has never forgotten the horrors he was forced to endure.

It was only when he heard of Denis Ryan's story that Terry decided to come forward and make contact with Denis. Denis and Terry remain friends today.

When I was growing up money was tight. I helped out my mother and father where I could. I'd snare rabbits, fish for trout in the local waterways, gather mushrooms in the inland rainforests and collect golf balls at the local golf course and sell them back to the golfers. The money I got from my hunting and gathering was sufficient to at least assist my parents in buying school uniforms and textbooks.

The golf course is bordered on one side by Bass Strait and on the other by the Catholic church, Our Lady of the Sea.

On one occasion, I was down at the golf course with a mate, Darrin, hunting for golf balls that had sliced and hooked into the rough.

We were used to golfers walking past while they played their games. Sometimes we'd approach them with an offer of a bag of balls for a few bob. But this time, the only man who approached us was a priest in his vestments. He introduced himself to us as Father John Day. He had a telescope on the balcony of the presbytery and asked us if we'd like to come up and have a look.

I'd never used a telescope before and I knew Darrin was keen to give it a go, so off we went with the priest.

We spent a little while looking through the telescope. Day kept his distance while Darrin was there but after we'd both taken a gander through it, Day asked Darrin to go home.

Darrin knew he wasn't welcome anymore. We both felt a little uneasy but Darrin took off as commanded.

Not long after he left, Day approached me, and stood over me. I remember he told me to relax and not make a sound.

He took off his gown and underwear and exposed his genitals to me. He grabbed my hand and placed it on his penis.

I was only 11 years old and I was terrified. I started crying and begged him to let me go home.

His manner changed quickly when he saw I was not going to be compliant.

'If you don't do as I tell you, I will ensure that your mother and father lose their jobs and you'll be sent to Tally-Ho.'

Tally-Ho was a boys' home in Melbourne. As kids we didn't know much about it except it was a place to be feared.

I didn't know much about Catholicism but I knew the power the clergy had in those days. If Day said he could do these things, I believed he could.

I was frightened and I let him do what he wanted.

That was the start of it, two and a half years of sexual abuse, torment, fear, constant nightmares and profound thoughts of suicide which prevail today.

Once a week I would go to the local youth club, a gym that was run by one of the local coppers. On so many occasions on the walk home, Day would turn up in one of his showy cars and tell me to get in. I remember the smell of him to this day. He stank of grog and body odour, of lust and depravity. I can close my eyes today and that smell will return and waft into my nostrils.

Put it down to a cruel trick of memory.

He had an eerie way of knowing wherever I was in Apollo Bay. I don't know how he did it. Sometimes, he found me in the bush, hunting rabbits, other times while I was just walking down a quiet road. It was as if he had a sixth sense. It added sharply to the fear I felt.

When he ordered me into his car, he'd drive up into the bush around the Barham River Flats. He would undress me and then undress himself and then hug me and the smell of the man would become sharp, leading me to feel ill, sick to the core. He would hug me and hold my buttocks so tightly that he caused bruising, then he would rape me. More often than not he'd bugger me. Sometimes he'd grab my head and force my mouth down on to his penis, choking me with it.

Afterwards he would leave me bleeding while he hurriedly got dressed. I'd be curled into a ball and would weep helplessly. Day didn't give a damn.

Rather he would tell me that he had boys just like me all over the place—in Lorne, Beech Forest, Mildura, Timboon and around Apollo Bay, too.

I never told a living soul about it, with the exception of my little black and white cocker spaniel, Milo. Milo was my constant companion in those days. After Day raped me and left me in the bush, Milo and I would go to a pool at the bottom of a waterfall, near where I used to trap rabbits. I would try and scrub the bruises from my body with an old scrubbing brush I kept there. I had an old singlet I hid under a rock and I used it to wash my anus and my private parts in the pool while Milo looked on. I'm sure that little dog knew why I was crying and what I was enduring.

Father Day was a cruel, sadistic, cunning and manipulative man. I'm sure that some of the parents in the town knew what he was up to, but out of fear or negligence, they didn't pipe up to protect the kids. I knew of at least five other boys that Day raped. There would have been many more.

I was raped by this man for almost three years. And every time, he would threaten and bully me into silence.

So at the age of 13, I took off. I could not stand it anymore. I ran away from Father Day, my parents, my family and my friends in Apollo Bay. It was all I could do to stop it.

That morning, Mum gave me a shilling to go to the store and buy some bread. I wandered down past the pier and saw a fishing boat, loading up ready to head out to sea. I spoke to the skipper and he told me that the boat was bound south. He offered me passage to the island if I did a few odd jobs on the boat.

I hid on the boat all day, terrified that Father Day would appear out of nowhere as he had so often done and bring my escape to an abrupt halt. And I'd be back up the bush again with him raping me.

For once, it didn't happen. Or perhaps I was too well hidden. I didn't tell my parents I was leaving. I didn't tell them for three weeks that I was alive and well. God only knows what they went through.

I was just too frightened that I'd be forced to come back. I waited three weeks before I asked a publican's wife to give Mum and Dad a call to tell them I was all right. When they asked me why I had run away, I couldn't say. I just told them I was having problems at school.

I didn't go back though. I couldn't. I was still in fear of Day and what he could do to me and my parents.

I stayed on there as a labourer on a work camp. It was a tough place and the older workers gave me regular hidings. Some of the older men used to play a game, a sort of Russian roulette with a rifle. There were some bloody cruel bastards among them. Still, anything was better than being raped by Father Day. And in a strange way, I felt free.

When I was 16, I was approached by a man I'd describe as a real Christian. He was a Methodist youth worker. He offered me the chance to return to school. I grabbed at the chance. I did pretty well at school, got my matric and headed out to the wide world.

I found I was a pretty good Australian Rules footballer. I played some good footy in the country and got asked to come down to Melbourne and play in the VFL. I played a few games. It was tough footy and I loved every minute of it.

Over the years I found that I could escape the deep feelings of guilt, fear and revulsion through alcohol. I became an alcoholic but I knew it was all due to the trauma I had suffered as a kid.

I found Alcoholics Anonymous and after a few lapses managed to stay sober. I've been sober now for twenty years.

I was married in 1971 and have three wonderful children, all of whom have developed into wonderful adults. I'd like to think that I offered them a loving and supportive environment. I love my children dearly.

I was divorced after eleven years of marriage. I found it very difficult to adjust to married life. It couldn't have been easy for my wife and, just like with my parents, I could not bring myself to tell her about the abuse I suffered as a child.

As I get older, I find my mind drifts back to those days at Apollo Bay and Father Day's abuse. I have tried forgiveness and that has helped, but the depression remains like an unwanted guest in my mind. The nightmares have continued and, if anything, have become more frequent as I have gotten older.

Having buried these painful thoughts at the back of my mind for so long, I find raking over them to be upsetting. I have had to maintain my Christian faith but find the word 'trust' makes me question my faith at times.

I was happy to assist with this book because I knew what a terrible treatment was handed out to Denis Ryan. He had tried to bring that mongrel Day to account, but ended up being forced out of the job that he loved. It was a terrible price to pay.

Others have paid an even more terrible price. It is my wish that this book will lead to Father Day's victims being remembered properly. Some, like me, have survived. Others have fallen hard into grog or just couldn't handle the trauma and took their own lives. I know at least three people who committed suicide in Apollo Bay, either death at their own hands or through reckless behaviour that was designed to lead to an untimely end. Anything to make the memories go away.

I've been asked what I'd do if I could front Father Day today. Would I want to get some of my own back? Would I want to confront him? It's all hypothetical. Sometimes I feel anger and resentment towards him but I dismiss these thoughts, knowing he is dead and before judgment. But if I could see him just once, the only thing I'd do is ask him, why?

Acknowledgments

We have sought the truth in the research and writing of this book and would like to thank many people for their assistance in finding it.

We would like to thank those victims of Day who came forward willingly to tell their stories. It is hoped that their courage in doing so will be rewarded with the knowledge that, finally, the truth will be known and understood.

We would also like to thank others who have invested their time and energy in assisting with this book: Police Association Victoria Secretary Greg Davies, Bryan Harding, John Howden, John Zigouras, Sharon Lapkin, Bill Hager, Russell Savage, George Baddeley, Alan Erskine, and Michael, Martin and Anthony Ryan.

Finally, we would like to thank our wives, Norma Ryan and Jennifer Hoysted, for their tireless support. Without them this book would not have come into being.

ACKNOWLEDGMENTS

This book is not intended to be an attack on the Roman Catholic Church. It's a plea for the Church itself to confront the truth; only then can reparation begin.

Let we, the congregation, be your confessor and your penance be the truth.

Index

A

Arnold, Rupert Henry, 94–5
Arundell, Father Daniel, 81
Ashton, Graham, 220
Atkinson, Tom, 21
Australian Federal Police, 42
Australian Labor Party (ALP), 62–3; see also Ryan, Denis
Australian Security Intelligence Organisation (ASIO), 65, 108, 170, 195; see also Barritt, Jim

B

Baker, Sid, 206
Barritt, Alma, 54, 194
Barritt, Barney, 46
Barritt, Denis 'Dinny', 44–6, 195
Barritt, Jim, viii, 10, 44–7, 50–3, 60, 64, 66, 68–9, 95, 101–6, 130, 152, 155, 159–61, 176, 179, 186, 201, 210, 241, 243
ASIO operative, as, 65–7, 108, 195
church building fund, 65, 75, 122, 126–7
Father John Day, protection of, 67, 69, 70–1, 88, 113, 168, 173, 216; see also Day, John Michael Joseph
Father John Day and Joe Kearney, relationship with, 71, 98–9, 113–14, 132, 139
moral character, 91–3, 194–5
policing techniques, 66, 95, 106–12
prize chickens, keeping of, 54–5
radio show, 61–2
SP bookies, relationship with, 125–6
war service, 55–9
Bates, John, 107

Bell, Clarrie, 13, 16–18, 20, 173
Blain, John, 121
Bolte, Sir Henry, 182
Braybrook, Ron, 214
Brewster, Lloyd, 46–7
Brodie, Bill, 54, 123–4, 138, 163, 185–6
Brown, Gil, 22
Bull, Bobby, 15
Burford, Kym, 142–5, 238–46

C

Cahill, Professor Des, 2
Carmichael, Jack, 180, 186, 191–2, 195–7, 200
Carruthers, Alfie, 42
Carton, Kevin, 36
Cashin, Pat, 214–15
Catholic Mafia, 133–49, 168–70, 179, 193, 199, 201, 203, 215, 223
Child, Harvey, 171–2, 174, 177–8, 187–8, 210–13
Child, Ray, 32, 41–2, 171
Clugston, Hugh, 42–3, 173
Connors, Peter, 218–19
Coombes, Allen, 20–1
Corpus Christi College, 2
Craig, Ernie 'The Harp', 42
Crowley, Bill, 193

D

Day, John Michael Joseph, viii, 1, 74, 128–9, 178, 180, 187–8, 204–5
   career, 2, 82, 94
   church building fund, 75, 122, 128
   confessional, violation of, 86–8
   Jim Barritt, association with, 52, 71, 113–14, 139, 146, 216
   Joseph Kearney, association with, 71, 113–14, 139, 157, 216
   moral character, 6, 79, 98–9, 132, 162
   police investigation of, 152, 178, 187–8, 192–5
   victims, 2–5, 118–20, 128, 137–41, 143–5, 150, 152, 156, 176–8, 180, 202–3, 210, 213, 216, 218, 221–2, 227–53
Deacon, Frank, 154–5
De Coursey Shaw, Dr, 40
Del Bollo, Father Anthony, 167
Democratic Labor Party (DLP), 63
Dillon, Sir John Vincent, 186–7, 191, 202
Don Bosco Youth Centre, 8
Duffy, Harry, 178, 191

INDEX

F
Fitzgibbon, John, 227–37
Foley, Alf, 207
Ford, Jack, 94, 169

G
Geracitano, Illario, 105–6
Geracitano, Teresa, 107
Glennon, Michael, 200
Grand Hotel, Mildura, 59, 177
Gribbin, Harry 'The Horse', 3, 26–9

H
Hager, Bill, 214–15
Hague, Jack, 36
Halloran, Father Laurie, 77, 81
Hamer, Sir Rupert, 181–2, 184, 186, 191, 206, 209
Hanrahan, Hazel, 15, 16, 18
Hardy, Frank, 169
Hayes, Joe, 68, 72, 91, 126–7
 Jim Barritt, attitude towards, 92–3, 194
Herbert, Harry, 147, 163
Herbert, Lynette, 147
Holding, Tim, 212
Holland, Frank, 36, 101, 104, 168
Hoover, J. Edgar, 53, 61, 67

Hotel Spencer (O'Connor's), Melbourne, 35–6, 39, 46, 101, 149
Howden, John, 136–8, 146, 156–60, 165, 177, 188, 198
Hower, Bill, 9

I
Irwin, Alby, 146–9, 151–6, 159–61, 168, 178–9, 184–6, 188–9, 191, 197–8, 201–2

J
Jackson, Reginald, 155, 178–9, 191–3, 195–6, 206, 214
Jacobson, Marty, 94
Jenkins, Thomas, 13–20, 36, 173

K
Kaye Abortion Inquiry, 94
Kearney, Joe, vii, 68, 71, 79, 88, 95, 98–9, 126, 176, 179, 241, 243
 alleged rape, 73, 132, 161, 177, 224
 clerk of courts, as, 72–3
 Father John Day and Jim Barritt, relations with, 71, 113–14, 139–40, 146, 148, 160, 216

rorting of court and parish
funds, 73–6, 120–3, 125,
127, 156–7, 177
Kelly, James, 30
Kelly, Ned, 29, 62
Kulenovic, Mustafa, 109

L

Lane, Sarah, 143
Lavarnos, John, 122–5
Leary, Jack, 183
Light, The, magazine, 204
Lind, Alan, 183, 186
Lynch, Terry, 121, 177

M

McAllister, Graham, 163
MacArdle, John, 207
McBride, Bill, 201–2
McGrath, Laurie, 153
McMenamin, Harry, 206
McPartland, Jack, 148–9, 154–6, 159–61, 166, 168, 178, 183
Mafia, 67
Mannix, Archbishop Daniel, 2, 19, 63, 65, 170
Mathews, Jack, 94
Meehan, Jack, 30–1, 68
Meehan, Kath, 68
Melbourne Observer, The, 205

Mitchell, Milton 'Mitch', 32–3
Mooney, Bill, 36
Mooney, Colin, 9–10
Mordialloc RSL, president of, 33–4
Mornane, Stan, 59
Mulkearns, Bishop Ronald Austin, 7–8, 82, 134, 158–61, 165, 175, 177–9, 204–5, 218
Murphy, Michael, 26–9
Murphy, Noel, 106–8

N

National Civic Council, 63
Nixon, Christine, 210–14
Noble, John, 161

O

O'Collins, Bishop James Patrick, 6–7, 82, 95–6, 132–4, 151
O'Connor, John 'Baton Jack', 102, 165, 169–80, 183, 187–200, 202–3, 205, 210–14
O'Connor, Leo, 35
O'Donnell, Michael, 67–71, 113

P

Park, Doug, 18
Pell, Cardinal George, 82, 205
Police Appeals Board, 198

INDEX

Police Association Victoria, The, 197–9
Pope Benedict XVI, 215
Pope Pius XI, 170
Power Without Glory, 169–70

R

Renwick, Dot, 15, 16, 18
Renwick, Eric, 15
Ridsdale, Father Gerald, 6–7, 9–10, 81–2, 85, 133–4, 162, 200, 216, 223
Rosengren, James, 8–9
Royal Commission into Institutional Responses to Child Sexual Abuse, 222
Russell, Fred, 34–9, 101, 149, 170
Ryan, Anthony, 77, 129, 164, 166–7, 208
Ryan, Denis
  Australian Labor Party, allegiance to, 63
  background and early career, 3, 11, 20, 22, 25, 41
  Catholic Mafia, invitation to join, 36–7, 170, 223
  faith, 20–1, 36, 77–8, 83–5, 165
  family, 39, 165
  Father John Day, encounters with, 1, 16–17, 50–2, 167, 173; *see also* Day, John Michael Joseph
  forced transfer/resignation of, 197, 200–1
  Frank Deacon, encounter with, 154–5
  Jim Barritt, working relationship with, 10, 51–2, 135, 151, 163
  job offers, 206–7
  local politics, career in, 209
  Mildura Manchester Unity Cricket Club, 102
  move to Mildura, 43, 48
  nightmares, 166, 224
  Police Association, appeal to, 197–9
  promotion to detective, 26
  Red Cliffs Players, involvement in, 130
  standing in Mildura community, 189
  Towards Healing process, 218–19
  victims' statements, collection of, 140, 144–5, 150, 152, 156, 158, 161–2, 176, 178–80, 198, 203
  Victoria Police force, cover up by, 168, 172–6, 180, 183, 187–202

Ryan, Emily, 3
Ryan, Francis, 3
Ryan, Gavin, 40, 48, 78, 97–9, 102, 129, 164, 166–7, 208
Ryan, Jean, 39–41, 43, 48–50, 91, 163, 166–7, 171–2, 199, 201
  breakdown, 207–8
  conversion to Catholicism, 77, 164
  family background, 163–4
Ryan, Martin, 40–1, 48, 78, 102, 129, 164, 166–7, 208
Ryan, Michael, 40–1, 43–4, 48, 78, 97, 99, 102, 129, 164, 166–7, 208
Ryan, Thomas, 11
Ryan, Tighe, 11

S

Sacred Heart Peace Memorial Church, Mildura, 167, 217
Sacred Heart Primary School, Mildura, 150, 156, 161, 176, 203, 239, 240, 244
Saker, Bob, 22–3
Salvation Army, The, 164
Santamaria, Bartholomew Augustine 'Bob', 63
Savage, Russell, 211–12, 214
Schulz, Constable, 214

Sheahan, Father Leslie, 81
Shilton, Les, 181–4, 206
Sister Claude, 228–9, 231–3
Sister Euphemia, 139
Sister Mary-Bernadette, 240
Sister Pancratius, 137, 140, 175
Special Branch (Victoria Police), 170
St Finbar's Church, Sans Souci, 3
St James Presbytery, Elsternwick, 187
St Joseph's Church, Red Cliffs, 166–7
St Joseph's College, Mildura, 96, 102, 136, 150, 156, 164, 175, 203, 243
St Joseph's Primary School, Red Cliffs, 164
St Patrick's Cathedral, Melbourne, viii, 8, 17, 19, 36–7, 63, 149, 224
Sunraysia Daily, The, 60

T

Taffe, Father Peter, 153
Tally-Ho Boys' Home, 249
Taylor, 'Fishy', 30–1
Teese, Eric, 101
'Terry', 247–53
Thomas, Jack, 103–5

INDEX

Tilley, George, 60
Towards Healing process, 217–19
Tripp, Don, 56–62, 64, 69–71, 88–93, 102, 113–17
Truth, The, 60

V

Volstead Act, 32

W

Walsh, Len, 46
Wilkes, Frank, 182
Wintersun Hotel, Mildura, 109, 141
Working Man's Club, Mildura, 56, 136, 142, 153, 163, 183
Wren, John, 170
Wright, Ken, 99–100